Praise for LIVING JESUS:

"Luke Timothy Johnson's new book does two fundamental things beautifully: it honors the word 'spirituality' in a seriously theological fashion and grounds that much-abused word in a full reading of the New Testament witness to the Risen Jesus. This accomplished work, wearing considerable learning lightly, deserves a wide readership." —LAWRENCE S. CUNNINGHAM, University of Notre Dame

"*Living Jesus* is many things: a brief but comprehensive New Testament introduction, a superb biblical foundation for courses on Jesus and christology, an exercise in biblical interpretation that masterfully illustrates and teaches interpretation, a testimony of faith that strengthens the faith of others. A challenging work destined to be controversial; many of us will remember it as a key work along the path of biblical scholarship's keeping and/or reowning of its soul."

—WILLIAM M. THOMPSON, Duquesne University

"This book is important. Johnson makes clear that there is more to Jesus than can be measured by the historian. Like John crying in the wilderness, this is a voice that needs to be heard. The implicit call is not only for repentance, but also for dialogue." —WILLIAM R. FARMER, University of Dallas, editor of *The International Bible Commentary*

"Proceeding from faith in the resurrected Jesus as living Spirit, Luke Timothy Johnson clearly sets out the classical modes of encountering that Jesus. Scripture, creeds, worship, and teaching are all depicted in their living, personal power within the church, in sharp contrast to a merely historical view of Jesus."

—BRUCE CHILTON, Bard College, author of *Pure Kingdom: Jesus' Vision of God*

"This book is frankly very important at this time: many good and well-intentioned Christians are losing the dynamism of a living Presence for mere mind games. Luke Timothy Johnson gives us the pattern and promise of the 'real thing.' I hope many read it and 'know.'"

—RICHARD ROHR, O.F.M., author of *Jesus' Plan for a New World*

LIVING JESUS

LIVING JESUS

Learning the Heart of the Gospel

❋

LUKE TIMOTHY JOHNSON

HarperSanFrancisco
A Division of HarperCollins*Publishers*

LIVING JESUS: *Learning the Heart of the Gospel*. Copyright © 1999 by Luke Timothy Johnson. All rights reserved. Printed in the United States of America. No part of this book may be used or reproduced in any manner whatsoever without written permission except in the case of brief quotations embodied in critical articles and reviews. For information address HarperCollins Publishers, 10 East 53rd Street, New York, NY 10022.

HarperCollins books may be purchased for educational, business, or sales promotional use. For information please write: Special Markets Department, HarperCollins Publishers, 10 East 53rd Street, New York, NY 10022.

HarperCollins Web Site: http://www.harpercollins.com

HarperCollins®, ♣®, and HarperSanFrancisco™
are trademarks of HarperCollins Publishers Inc.

FIRST EDITION

Library of Congress Cataloging-in-Publication Data

Johnson, Luke Timothy.
    Living Jesus : learning the heart of the Gospel / Luke Timothy
Johnson. — 1st ed.
    Includes index.
    ISBN 0-06-064282-3 (cloth)
    ISBN 0-06-064283-1 (pbk.)
    1. Jesus Christ—Resurrection. 2. Bible. N.T. Gospels—History
and Criticism. 3. Jesus Christ—Biography—History and criticism.
4. Jesus Christ—Historicity. 5. Jesus Christ—History of
doctrines—20th century. I. Title.
BT481.J64 1998
232'.5—dc21   98-22647
                                            CIP

99 00 01 02 03 RRD(H) 10 9 8 7 6 5 4 3

To Joy
Partner, Lover, Friend

Contents

Preface

In this book I venture to think through the implications of a strong belief that the real Jesus is the living, resurrected Jesus and that being a Christian means modeling one's life on that Jesus as best we can. In that sense it is a less polemical and more constructive sequel to my recent publication, *The Real Jesus*. The earlier book took on the cultural phenomenon of Jesus in the nightly news. This one reflects on the mystery of the person of Jesus as good news.

I have written this book for people who, like me, find much of what is called spirituality too far removed from traditional Christian faith, and much of what is written about Jesus too little concerned with the transformation of human freedom. Calling anything a spirituality these days is an invitation to misunderstanding, since there are so many varieties afloat. Readers should not look here for a how-to manual for psychic renewal or reassurance. Nor should they expect a rendering of Jesus that enables a casting off of ecclesiastical manacles. Spirituality here means not the cultivation of the human spirit, but the response of human freedom to the Holy Spirit of God. For Christians, this encounter involves the person of Jesus, not as a historical figure of the past, but as resurrected Lord in the present.

But how can such an encounter with Jesus be conceived? Is there a place between a historicism that wants to keep Jesus locked in his past and a mysticism that threatens to vaporize the particularity of Jesus altogether? I try to locate that place in a process of intersubjective learning within the community of faith—a process in which the diverse portrayals of Jesus in the writings of the New Testament play a positive rather than a negative role. This book does not pretend to enact such a process but instead seeks to encourage an appreciation for its several dimensions.

LUKE TIMOTHY JOHNSON
CANDLER SCHOOL OF THEOLOGY
EMORY UNIVERSITY
APRIL 1, 1998

PART 1

The Truth That Is in Jesus

CHAPTER 1

He Is the Living One

It makes a big difference whether we think someone is dead or alive. To the person in either of those conditions it probably makes an even bigger difference. But it certainly also matters to anyone interested in that person.

When someone is dead, even someone we knew alive, we may be able to learn more about him or her as time goes by. If the person was famous, accomplishments or words will continue to circulate. Diligent research might uncover proof of actual deeds and words, and we can also discover how these were perceived and interpreted by those who survive. But the only way we will hear from the actual person again is if some previously undiscovered deed or unpublished word is made public. And even then, we say, "I didn't know she thought that back then. How interesting." We hear about it now, but the information is about someone no longer here: an echo from the past, not a new word in the present.

When we think someone is alive, we have a completely different set of expectations. People who are alive are still capable of doing new things and saying new things. They can change their minds. They can show up in different places from the ones they used to inhabit. They can surprise us. They can appear on our doorstep, contact us in the middle of a family celebration, arrive at our bedside when we are sick. Even if we are separated from a living person for a long period of time, or circumstances keep us far apart, we are able to say, "She is my friend," or "He is my brother," in a way different not only in tone but also in meaning from the way we say, "She was my mother," or "He was my teacher," about someone who has died.

When someone is still living and we are in relationship with that person, our knowledge of the person is more multiform than in the case of someone dead. In addition to the documentary record and the memories of others—data available to us about *all* people, living and dead—new data is still coming in. It is possible to address a living person and ask, "What did you mean by that?" or "Do you still think that?" and expect an answer. In the presence of this person, furthermore, we can observe how she acts with others. Even more important, we can experience how she acts toward and with us. As a result of this continued contact, knowledge of the living person grows and changes. The process of learning is therefore much more complicated.

The dead, on the other hand, stay still. Their deeds are ended; their words are complete; their power—however impressive it may once have been—is gone. Others have quite literally taken their place, walking over the spot where they lie buried. They neither move nor complain. An adequate historical reconstruction of the dead is therefore a goal realizable at least in principle, although—depending on the information available for analysis—often extraordinarily difficult to achieve. We know how frequently historical perspectives even on the recent dead change in response to new information and changing criteria for evaluation. But ideally at least, historians can hope to fix an account of a person truly dead, finally in the past.

The most important question concerning Jesus, then, is simply this: Do we think he is dead or alive?

If Jesus is simply dead, there are any number of ways in which we can relate ourselves to his life and his accomplishments. And we might even, if some obscure bit of data should turn up, hope to learn more about him. But we cannot reasonably expect to learn more *from* him.

If he is alive, however, everything changes. It is no longer a matter of our questioning a historical record, but a matter of our being put in question by one who has broken every rule of ordinary human existence. If Jesus lives, then it must be as life-giver. Jesus is not simply a figure of the past in that case, but a person in the present; not merely a memory that we can analyze and manipulate, but an agent who can confront and instruct us. What we learn *about* him must therefore include what we continue to learn *from* him.

To be a Christian means to assert that Jesus is alive, is indeed life-giving Spirit (1 Cor. 15:45). To consider Jesus simply as a figure of the past means to consider Jesus not from the perspective of a Christian but from that of one who stands outside Christian conviction. The Christian prays, "Come, Lord Jesus" (Rev. 22:20; see 1 Cor. 16:22), intending thereby to address a real and living person capable of manifesting his presence still more palpably. Such a prayer is nonsensical to one who is not a Christian, for it is fantasy to address the dead as though still alive. It is either make-believe or necromancy to summon from a grave one who died two thousand years ago.

This seems to be one of those very few choices that allow no equivocation. There is no middle ground between dead and alive. If Jesus is dead, then his story is completed. If he is alive, then his story continues.

The decision whether to consider Jesus dead or alive ought to have consequences for how we regard his story. If his story continues after his death, then paying attention only to what he did before his death is at best inadequate, at worst fundamentally distorting. For if Jesus is alive, then he is alive not simply as a continuation of his former existence (as a wraith or poltergeist might be) but as the one who has entered into God's own life and who rules creation as its Lord.

To be a Christian, then, means confessing that Jesus is alive in the sense of that ancient declaration, "Jesus is Lord" (1 Cor. 12:3; Rom. 10:9; Phil. 2:11). The statement could scarcely be simpler, but it requires for its sincere enunciation a firm decision concerning both how one regards Jesus and consequently how one regards one's own life. "Jesus is Lord" is what is called a *performative* statement—that is, a statement that finds its sense not only as a declaration about reality but as a declaration concerning how the speaker really lives.

Coming to grips with the implications of the confession is more complex. What sort of life is it that Jesus now lives? How can we speak meaningfully of his continuing presence? How does he manifest himself? How can we both speak of Jesus' presence and pray that he come again? Theology does its best to sort through all these corollaries of confession.

The essential point, though, is that the confession of Jesus as resurrected, as living with God's own life, and as ruling as Lord of the church and world is what distinguishes the Christian view of Jesus from every other view. For everyone else, Jesus is another dead man; for Christians, he is the Living One. This confession is implicit in the very existence of a church gathered in Jesus' name, in its celebration of the Lord's Supper, in its healing in the name of Jesus, in its struggle against evil for the little ones with whom Jesus identifies himself.

As now, so in the beginning. Despite the efforts of some contemporary scholars to hypothesize forms of a "Jesus movement" that continued after his death with no belief in his resurrection, there is no positive evidence for any such movement. Our earliest Christian writings are diverse in many and important respects, but they are in agreement on this point: Jesus who was crucified is now the living Lord. Great and convoluted effort is required to detect any hint of a Jesus movement lacking belief in the resurrection. In contrast, the evidence to support the proposition that Christianity was birthed by the resurrection faith is displayed everywhere in the pages of the New Testament and is overwhelmingly attested by the Christian tradition.

If, as Christians claim, Jesus is powerfully alive as Lord, then our "learning Jesus" appropriately begins with that premise and not another. Before developing more fully the implications of the confession that Jesus is among the living, therefore, it is useful to note the inadequacy of another premise for learning Jesus.

The Historian's Jesus Is the Dead Jesus

If Jesus is simply a figure of the past whose existence ceased with his human death, then the historian's craft is the appropriate path to knowing Jesus. What can be known about him must be learned in the same way we learn about any other figure of the past, which is to study what he said and did until his death. Some attention might be given to his ongoing influence and to the movement that arose after him, but if he is dead, then *Jesus'* story ends with his death. The story of the church, in that case, is really a story about other people, not Jesus.

One can scarcely complain if someone who is not a Christian should want to study Jesus historically in the same way that she would study Napoleon or Michelangelo, operating on the premise that finding the "historical Jesus" is a matter of analyzing events during his human lifetime. One would applaud her taking great pains to distinguish, insofar as she was able, between "what really happened" and the sorts of legendary accretions that grow up around figures who stand at the head of religious movements.

Although her task would make sense, given her premise that Jesus is a dead person of the past, the possibilities of success for her historical reconstruction of Jesus would be dim indeed. The obstacles to the historical study of all ancient figures are severe: sources are slender, they are selective, and they show extensive bias. Advancing against such obstacles is not easy even for scholars researching characters who everyone agrees have stayed dead! Arguments remain lively concerning such relatively well documented figures as Socrates and Caesar and Cicero, for example.

But in the case of Jesus—apart from a few casual acknowledgments by Jewish and Greco-Roman authors concerning his existence, his death, and the movement that continued after him (notices of great importance to any historian, to be sure)—everything we know was written by people who did *not* think he was dead, but alive and powerfully present among them. And everything they wrote about Jesus was written from this post-resurrection perspective. For them his story was not over but was only beginning.

Even if our hypothetical non-Christian historian were a great scholar and exercised the most exquisite discipline and care, we would not be sanguine about her findings, for the difficulties are indeed daunting. One early and formidable hurdle she would face is one that all historians before her have faced: what to make of the Gospels? She could rely heavily on the narrative framework of the Gospels, making judicious choices between them when they disagreed and lightly correcting them for theological bias; or she could dismantle the narrative structure of the Gospels completely, trying to salvage from those stories historically more plausible pieces and fitting those bits back into an alternative framework drawn from broad historical probabilities or a comparative analysis.

In the first case, she would be left with the question of whether the resulting picture was sufficiently critical: Had she merely retold the Bible story and designated it History? In the second case, she would wonder whether the reconstruction was not a projection driven by her need to have Jesus appear one way rather than another: Was her Jesus another example of T. A. Manson's aphorism, "By their lives of Jesus ye shall know them"?

If it makes sense for someone who begins with the premise that Jesus is dead to seek knowledge of him through historical investigation, then it also makes sense for a Christian—someone who believes with all her heart that Jesus is truly the Resurrected One and lives powerfully as Lord—to adopt the same position methodologically: to undertake a functional bracketing of her personal conviction in order to enter into conversation with other people of good will who cannot share her belief but who are still obviously interested in what can be known about Jesus as a human person. In order to enter that conversation, our believer can legitimately play a "what if" game.

She can pretend, for the sake of her historian's craft, that in fact she does not consider Jesus to be alive. For the sake of her historical project, she can decide to address herself only to those parts of the historical record that all investigators of good will and decent historical training might regard as pertinent. Thus, for the sake of this exercise, she would engage the traditions about Jesus' wonder-working not from the perspective of a believer who celebrates them as the anticipation of that inbreaking of God's rule that was the resurrection, but solely in terms of Jesus' reputation as a healer and the possibility—given the proper spiritual and psychosomatic conditions—that such healings happen. This approach to Jesus also makes sense, even if for the believer it is of limited usefulness and may actually be distorting. (If we act as if someone were dead even as an exercise, it can become a habit.)

Far less intelligible is the attempt by those who consider themselves to be Christians to secure a historical reconstruction of Jesus precisely to shape, or reshape, Christian faith. Such an effort uses an approach appropriate to the study of a dead person (the historical method) in order to rectify a community's convictions concerning a person it regards as alive, and does so purportedly from within that community. This is a very odd combination. Yet it is exactly the combination that has characterized the entire "quest for the historical Jesus" since the late eighteenth century—a quest engaged in not by secular scholars but almost entirely by Christian scholars (indeed, by Christian scholars who for the most part have also considered themselves to be *theologians*). The fact that this search has continued to our own day, despite its inherent difficulties and despite the widely disparate portraits of Jesus that have emerged from the efforts of scholars using comparable methods on basically the same materials, suggests that the quest for the historical Jesus has been, from its inception, more about theology than about history.

The basic premise of the quest is that the church that confesses that Jesus is alive and (sharing in God's own life) powerfully if invisibly present to creation as its Lord is mistaken. Furthermore, the church's error goes all the way back to the beginning, so that the Gospels themselves, written as they are from the perspective of the resurrection, distort who Jesus really was in his humanity. Traditional (creedal) Christianity should therefore be corrected by historical research that can recover the "real" Jesus. The community's developed sense of the living person that it continues to experience in its midst should not be the measure of Christian identity; rather, that measure should be a corrected account of Jesus' deeds and words before his death.

It would take considerable effort to uncover the precise theological perceptions that underlie this premise. But it is abundantly clear that those perceptions include the view that a Christianity based explicitly on the resurrection of Jesus is wrong. Perhaps this is because proponents of the historical approach think of Christianity as a way of life based on certain ideals or social principles rather than as a religious response to supernatural power. Or perhaps they consider the time of Jesus' ministry to be a unique revelation of the incarnate God, such that it was what Jesus really said and did rather than what the church remembered of him that remains normative for Christian life. Whatever the underlying perceptions, those favoring the historical approach conclude that even if there was a resurrection, it is not defining of Christianity. Christianity should therefore be shaped by what historical research can recover about a dead man.

I must confess that this last option makes little sense to me, despite my general appreciation of the historical approach. I know that highly intelligent people have been involved in such efforts, and that many of them have had both good will and the sincere desire to reform Christianity on the basis of their historical findings. But as far as I can tell, the only way they can be truly consistent in their thinking is if they say clearly, "Traditional Christianity based on the living presence of Jesus in the world is wrong." If they speak so clearly, they identify themselves as working from a basis fundamentally different from that of the New Testament itself, and their program of reforming Christianity on a new basis can be evaluated for what it really is. But as long as they *both* claim to hold Christian faith *and* seek to base that faith on a historically reconstructed Jesus, they are self-contradictory.

My present theme, however, is not the way of knowing the dead Jesus pursued by history, but the way of learning the living Jesus appropriate to faith. In order to develop this complex and critical investigation, it is helpful to begin where Christian faith itself begins—with the resurrection of Jesus—for the clear grasp of what faith claims here is essential for everything else that follows.

The Jesus of Faith Is the Living Jesus

Faith begins with the resurrection of Jesus in two ways. First, the resurrection is the grounding for the entire Christian life; if Jesus be not raised, as Paul tells the Corinthians, then our faith is in vain (1 Cor. 15:14). Second, the resurrection is the chronological beginning of the Christian religion; whatever loyalty and devotion Jesus aroused in his followers during his ministry was, according to the record, insufficient to prevent their betrayal, denial, and abandonment of him at his death. The "Jesus movement" ended with Jesus' death, but it started up again after his resurrection. It did so not in simple continuity with a previous ministry that was limited by the constraints of Jesus' physical capabilities, but with an even more important element of discontinuity marked by the way in which Jesus was now alive.

To measure the way in which the resurrection faith is the grounding for Christians in every age, then, it is entirely appropriate to begin with the testimony of those for whom the resurrection was in very fact the start of a new way of life: the writers of the New Testament. We can approach the mystery of the resurrection by asking the same question twice, each time with a slightly different emphasis: In what sense is Jesus *alive,* and in what sense is *Jesus* alive?

The answers to these questions provided by the New Testament itself are not precise, systematic, or entirely satisfactory to those seeking the resolution of a problem rather than the celebration of a mystery. Before seeking what precision and system is available, then, I need to remind myself and the reader that the compositions to which we turn were written for purposes other than answering these questions. The experience we seek to examine was for the authors of the New Testament the mysterious premise of their existence. Their speech about the resurrection, therefore, is most often allusive, indirect, and densely symbolic. I think that the writers of the New Testament would not have understood "the resurrection" as a separate topic about which one could speak; for them it was rather the all-encompassing reality into which they had been caught up. Their language sought to express a reality for which no language, nor any precedent experience except creation itself, provided analogy.

IN WHAT SENSE IS JESUS *ALIVE?*

The resurrection of Jesus has nothing to do with his avoiding death by luck or design in order to continue his former life without any real change. Theories ancient and modern proposing otherwise replace evidence with imagination. They also fail to appreciate that such a prosaic denouement would have been good news only for Jesus and his associates, not an event that changed the world. The New Testament is unswerving in its insistence that Jesus truly died—indeed, was killed by the legal violence of state execution (therefore in a certified and public way)—and was buried in the manner of others who had their lives ended. Like every other human being who ever lived, therefore, Jesus of Nazareth also died.

In the same way, the resurrection of Jesus is understood not as a resuscitation from clinical death, though such dramatic resuscitations are attested in the ancient world as well as in our own. Elijah raised the widow of Sarepta's son in this way so that the young man could continue his life (1 Kings 17:17–24). Jesus likewise raised the widow of Naim's son from his bier (Luke 7:11-16) and his friend Lazarus from the tomb (John 11:38-44). In all these cases, resurrection meant only the perpetuation of the same life that was led before the moment of death. Lazarus did not live in a qualitatively different fashion after being brought back to life. He was not more alive than before, simply alive again in the same way as before. That he was alive again no doubt pleased both Jesus and Lazarus's sisters, Mary and Martha. But even when resuscitated, Lazarus remained mortal; he still faced inevitable death. In other words, his mortality was postponed but not transcended. And when he finally died, Lazarus stayed dead, like all others before him. In sum, his resuscitation did not mean that he was more alive than he had been, or that he continued in life forever, or that he lived powerfully in the lives of others.

Nor is Jesus' life after his death, according to the New Testament, to be equated with the ways of "persisting in the world" that often apply to other humans who have died. He does not live on simply in the memory of loved ones, for example. Jesus is remembered within the community, to be sure, but there is no suggestion that these memories constitute his present existence; rather, his present activity complicates the process of remembering his "past" in ways that continue to befuddle those historians who wish to distinguish between them. Jesus is not "alive" merely as a dimension of the psychic life of others.

Nor is his life after death a matter of others continuing to teach what he taught. That too would be a kind of immortality, and not an unworthy one: it is, after all, the immortality enjoyed by Plato and Aquinas as long as each shall be read or studied. The New Testament text that comes closest to suggesting that Jesus' words perpetuate his presence is found at the end of Matthew's Gospel, when Jesus tells his disciples to "make learners of all nations, teaching them to observe all that I have commanded you." But even this statement concludes with the words "for behold *I am with you always* until the close of the age" (Matt. 28:20).

Jesus' life after death is not simply a matter of his being applied to later circumstances as a moral exemplar, in the way that the hero Herakles was invoked by the moral teacher Epictetus—even though the pattern of Jesus' life certainly is offered as an example to be imitated by Christians. Nor is the activity of Christians "in the name of Jesus" merely the association of present actions with an eponymous hero of the past, as is the case when people think of themselves as "Jeffersonian Democrats" or "Trotskyite Socialists." Moral examples and the ideals of heroes do indeed "live on" in some ways, but the heroes themselves are dead. Precisely because the New Testament's language about the living Jesus includes "living on" language about his memory, teaching, moral example, and name, it is important to recognize that these expressions are not to be identified with the central conviction concerning Jesus, which has to do not with the persistence of some aspect of his past, but above all with his personal presence in the present. The conviction of the New Testament writers is that he is somehow present among them, not simply that they are relating themselves to a figure of the past.

The resurrection of Jesus as it is understood in the writings of the New Testament is not only something that occurred to Jesus in the past; it is also something that continues to occur to others in the present. For example, Jesus appears to Paul years after his death: "Last of all, as to one born out of season, he appeared also to me" (1 Cor. 15:8). Paul claims to be a firsthand witness to the resurrection: "Am I not free, am I not an apostle, have I not seen our Lord Jesus?" (1 Cor. 9:1). Note that Paul calls him "Lord Jesus." The title "Lord" is for Paul precisely the designation of Jesus' *present* status in power.

Paul can say, "I have seen Jesus—as Lord," even though he was not a follower of Jesus on Easter Sunday or the days after; he was, in fact, a persecutor of Jesus' followers. Because of that, Paul's encounter with Jesus on the road to Damascus is of primary importance for our understanding of the resurrection as something far more than a physical resuscitation. When the Paul who was tormenting the messianic community is confronted by a living power that asks, "Saul, why are you persecuting *me*?" he asks; "Who are you, Lord?" knowing in the power of the experience itself that he is face to face with a personal transcendent power. The voice answers, "I am Jesus, whom you are persecuting" (Acts 9:4–5). Thus the resurrection is not a continuation of Jesus' former life, but is his entry into a new mode of existence that is more powerful, more "alive," than before. It is, indeed, Jesus' entry into the life of God, his "enthronement at the right hand of God," his establishment as "Lord" (see Acts 2:32–36).

As Lord, and as one who shares God's own life, Jesus exists not simply as a "living being" but as the very power of life: "The first man Adam became a living soul; the last Adam became a life-giving Spirit" (1 Cor. 15:45). The Holy Spirit is the mode of Jesus' resurrection presence to the world: "Now the Lord is the Spirit. And where the Spirit of the Lord is, there is freedom. And we all, gazing on the glory of the Lord with unveiled face, are being transformed into the same image from glory to glory, just as from the Lord who is Spirit" (2 Cor. 3:17–18).

The New Testament writings consistently make the connection between Jesus' entering into a participation in God's rule as Lord and the outpouring of the Holy Spirit on Jesus' followers. John notes that during Jesus' ministry "there was as yet no Spirit, for Jesus had not yet been glorified" (John 7:39): the Spirit was to be given after Jesus' elevation to the Father's presence (16:7–15), and was in truth breathed on his followers by Jesus after his resurrection (20:22). Luke has Peter declare at Pentecost, "This Jesus God has raised up, of which we are all witnesses; exalted to the right hand of God, and receiving the promise that is the Holy Spirit from the Father, he has poured out this which you are seeing and hearing" (Acts 2:32–33). For Paul, Jesus is established as "son of God in power by the spirit of holiness on the basis of the resurrection from the dead" (Rom. 1:4), and the confession "Jesus is Lord" is possible only "in the Holy Spirit" (1 Cor. 12:3).

If we say that the Holy Spirit is the mode through which the risen

Jesus is present to the world, we are not yet saying enough, but we are saying something real. The symbol "Spirit" in these writings, first of all, does not suggest a weak, derivative, vestigial sort of existence, as it might in a postenlightenment world in which *spirit* and *spiritual* tend to connote "ideal" rather than "real," mental rather than physical. In the symbolic world of the New Testament, the opposite is the case: the realm of Spirit is regarded as more real and powerful and "substantial" than the world of materiality. This is all the more true when the adjective *Holy* is attached to *Spirit*, denoting that the source and nature of this power are divine.

The symbol "Holy Spirit" communicates that aspect of Jesus' resurrection life that enables his personal existence to extend beyond the boundaries of his former physical body into the world. Transcendence is a function of Spirit. The power within humans to reach beyond their physical frames into the minds and hearts of others through knowledge and love is a pale intimation of what "Holy Spirit" means when used of God, whose transcendence is marked by the capacity to be interior to all existence simultaneously, and present to all that is created without ever being defined by creation, without ever ceasing to be Other to all the sensible round of being. Because Jesus' present existence has just that transcendent quality, the New Testament can use language that in purely physical terms would be impossible. In a single chapter of the Letter to the Romans, Paul speaks of those who are "in Christ Jesus" (8:1), talks of "the Spirit of life in Christ Jesus" (8:2), says that "the Spirit of God dwells in you" (8:9), outlines the consequences for "anyone who does not have the Spirit of Christ" (8:9) as well as for those who have Christ "in you" (8:10), and asserts that "if the Spirit of him who raised Jesus from the dead dwells in you, he who raised Jesus from the dead will give life to your mortal bodies also through his Spirit which dwells in you" (8:11). Such language of mutual presence and interiority, of "indwelling" (to use John's language again), is possible only in the realm of transcendence, which is the realm of Spirit.

To claim that Jesus is "life-giving Spirit," then, is to claim that Jesus now shares God's own capacity to be present in a way more instant and immediate than is possible to any merely mortal body, whose spirit is confined by the limits of physical capability and location. It means that the Jesus who before his death was, like all humans, circumscribed in his power to reach other humans is now no longer so limited. The symbolism of being "elevated to the right hand of God" is one way of expressing this reality, for to be at "God's right hand" is not to be in one place as opposed to another, but to share in God's power to be in *every* place as ruler. The language in John's Gospel about Jesus being "glorified" and "lifted up" after his death is likewise empowering: by resurrection Jesus shares in "God's glory"—that is, he partakes in the mode of being that is unique to God. As Paul says in Romans 14:8b–9, "[W]hether we live or whether we die, we are the Lord's. For to this end Christ died and lived again, that he might be Lord both of the dead and the living" (RSV).

It is Jesus' exalted mode of life as Lord, therefore, that legitimates turning to him in prayer, gathering and healing and preaching "in his name," and awaiting his return to judge the living and the dead with God's own authority. But that brings us to the next question.

IN WHAT SENSE IS *JESUS* ALIVE?

The New Testament's testimony that the risen Jesus exists in a new and more powerful way—a way discontinuous with his previously circumscribed humanity—is matched by its insistence that it is truly *Jesus* who exists in this fashion, and that his new life is also continuous with his previous one in that it truly extends his personal presence in the world.

Such insistence is all the more important to the degree that we (properly) emphasize the *Spirit* as the mode of Jesus' new life, for without careful attention to what the New Testament actually says, it is possible to evaporate Jesus' particular personhood into a generalized "spiritual force" or "cosmic spirit" so discontinuous with his mortal humanity as to render it nugatory.

The body is the symbol for both the continuity and the discontinuity of Jesus' presence in the world. That Jesus had a body in his mortal existence is obvious. But the mode of his bodily existence after resurrection is a slippery subject indeed, not least because any discussion involving the body as primary symbol of the self quickly reveals just how little most discussants hold in common. The question of what we mean by Jesus' body before and after the resurrection is complicated by the unreflective and overly confident assumptions we bring to it—assumptions that we know what we mean when we talk about our own bodies! In fact, any living body is at least as much a mystery as it is a problem. While a dead body is nothing more than a problem to be solved, a living body is a mystery to engage, whether it is the body that we inhabit (or that inhabits us) or the body of the resurrected Messiah.

Two extreme positions distort the classical Christian understanding of Jesus' resurrection. The first extreme places such emphasis on the note of discontinuity that any language about Jesus' body appears as merely formal and abstract. The second extreme places such emphasis on the continuity of Jesus' bodily existence that the resurrection comes dangerously close to being understood as the resuscitation of a corpse. The best way to avoid these extremes may be to follow as closely as possible the delicate and complex language of the New Testament itself as it seeks to communicate its conviction concerning the fact that (and the way in which) it is truly *Jesus* who lives.

When Paul is asked to deal with the question, "How are the dead raised? With what kind of body do they come?" his immediate response is the scornful, "You foolish person!" (1 Cor. 15:35–36). His point is that the good news (1 Cor. 15:12) is a *mystery* in which Jesus' followers have been caught up (1 Cor. 15:51), not a problem capable of solution by means of ordinary human calculation. But he goes on to emphasize the radical disparity between a natural and a glorified body (15:36–42), concluding with these words:

> So it is with the resurrection of the dead. What is sown is perish-
> able, what is raised is imperishable. It is sown in dishonor, it is
> raised in glory. It is sown in weakness, it is raised in power. It is sown
> a physical body, it is raised a spiritual body. . . . [J]ust as we have
> borne the image of the man of dust, we shall also bear the image of
> the man from heaven. I tell you this, brethren: flesh and blood cannot
> inherit the kingdom of God, nor does the perishable inherit the im-
> perishable. Lo, I tell you a mystery. We shall not all sleep but we shall
> all be changed. . . . [T]he dead will be raised imperishable and we
> shall be changed. For this perishable nature must put on the im-
> perishable and this mortal nature put on immortality. (1 Cor. 15:
> 42–53, RSV)

Paul tells us that "Christ has been raised from the dead, the first fruits of those who have fallen asleep" (1 Cor. 15:20, RSV). It follows from this that just as the bodies of all humans must be changed from mortal to immortal, from perishable to imperishable, from physical to spiritual, in order to inherit God's rule, so also must Jesus' body first have undergone precisely that transformation.

Paul's discourse suggests that any language about the resurrection body of Jesus must not only maintain the tension between continuity and discontinuity (it is really Jesus, but in a dramatically new way); it must also be willing to conceive of Jesus' glorified body (and therefore his presence to the world) in unanticipated ways.

The Gospel accounts of Jesus' postresurrection appearances have just that delicacy and allusiveness when speaking about Jesus' bodily presence. In contrast to the empty-tomb stories (Mark 16:1–8; Matt. 28:1–8; Luke 24:1–11; John 20:1–10), which emphasize that Jesus is no longer among the dead but is among the living—or, as Luke puts it, is "the Living

One"—these appearance accounts (Mark 16:9–20; Matt. 28:9–20; Luke 24:13–49; John 20:11–21:23) emphasize Jesus' presence among his immediate followers after his death.

On the one hand, some of the appearance accounts stress the reality of Jesus' physicality in order to show that it really *is* Jesus and none other whom the disciples encounter (John 20:26–28 and especially Luke 24:39–43).

On the other hand, Jesus' body is not by any means the same as it was before his death: the resurrected Jesus can appear to the disciples in the guise of a stranger on the road (Luke 24:13–32), for example, or be mistaken for a gardener (John 20:15–16); he can appear suddenly at a meal (Mark 16:14; Luke 24:36–43; John 21:9–14); he can pass through locked doors (John 20:19); and he can ascend skyward (Mark 16:19; Luke 24:53; Acts 1:9–11). Nor is "touching" Jesus' body unproblematic. In Matthew's Gospel, the women departing the tomb and encountering Jesus "touch his feet and worship him" (Matt. 28:9); but in John's Gospel, Mary is prevented by Jesus from holding him, "for I have not yet gone up to the Father" (John 20:17), and when Thomas is invited to touch Jesus' wounds, he does not actually do so but cries out, "My Lord and my God" (John 20:27–28). In the postresurrection appearances of Acts, it is difficult to know how to assess the bodily dimension of Stephen's vision of "Jesus standing at the right hand of God" (Acts 7:55) or Paul's encounter with a blinding light and commanding voice (Acts 9:3–4). Taken together, these passages suggest that the one who was resurrected is unquestionably the Jesus who died, and that his relationship to his body and to the world is infinitely more protean and pluriform than can be expressed in terms applicable to other embodied persons.

The sequence of postresurrection accounts found in Luke's Gospel and Acts expresses both continuity and discontinuity. Luke extends the resurrection experience through narrative stages in a way unparalleled in other Gospels. It is a mistake, I think, to take his narrative as a literal rendering of events in temporally discrete fashion. Luke attempts, rather, to capture the richness and complexity of the resurrection experience by four kinds of stories. Taken in sequence, these stories express the dialectic of continuity and discontinuity, of absence and presence, that lies at the heart of Christian conviction concerning Jesus after his death.

Luke's empty-tomb account (24:1–8) is a remarkably complex composition, especially when compared to its parallels in Mark and Matthew. In Luke, we find no statement concerning a future appearance. Instead, the women visiting the tomb are told that they are mistaken in their quest: "Why do you seek the Living One among the dead?" (24:5). It is clear from this response that Jesus' body is no longer where it had been, but this absence is explained on the basis of his being "the Living One," who cannot be constrained even by death. The women, however, are given no immediate vision of Jesus as alive. They are rather told to "remember" the words he had spoken in his past life concerning his death and resurrection (24:6). His "absence," then, is pregnant. The tomb is not entirely empty. Jesus' past life is over, yet it persists in the memory of those who will shortly come to understand that he truly is "the Living One," and their every memory of his past will be shaped by that growing realization of who he truly was all along.

The appearances in Luke 24:13–49 are obviously a mode not of Jesus' absence but of his presence to his followers. He moves about him as he had before—yet, as we have seen, not *really* as before. Jesus is not present in the way he had been when he walked and talked with them in Galilee. His presence to them now is both more powerful and more allusive, more dramatic and more mediated. Though he is "really" present in his body, that body has a transfigured quality that enables him to be present in different places to different people (24:31–34).

Luke's two ascension accounts (Luke 24:51 and Acts 1:9–11) serve to remove Jesus' body from the sight of humans as preparation for another mode of his presence. This is a deeper level of absence than the empty tomb, for it means that even as the Living One, Jesus will no longer be present in the sort of bodily shape that his disciples knew. That earlier mode of bodily presence was still limited. If Jesus ascends to the right hand of God and receives from him the promise of the Holy Spirit, then the "life" that is at work in him can be poured out over all humans, so that his presence can be mediated in all the ways in which those led by his Spirit body forth. Thus Luke's Pentecost account in Acts 2:1–5 is truly the climactic and decisive symbolization of the resurrection of Jesus, as Peter's speech makes clear: it is because God has made him both Christ and Lord by sitting him at God's right hand that Jesus can pour out the Spirit on all flesh (Acts 2:33–36). Absent from the dead, present in a new bodily form to a few, absent in body altogether, present more powerfully to all flesh: Luke's sequence of stories exquisitely expresses the truth that is in Jesus.

How, then, does Jesus now find continuing embodiment as life-giving Spirit? As all-powerful Lord, in any fashion he chooses! Jesus remains capable of surprise. But the ways in which Christians have come to recognize the face of the living Christ exist mainly within that assembly of those gathered in the name of Jesus who have drunk of the Spirit and have become "the body of Christ" (Rom. 12:5; 1 Cor. 6:14; 12:12–27; Eph. 1:23; 2:16; 4:4–16; 5:23, 30; Col. 1:18, 24; 2:17–19). Jesus is embodied in the texts that speak of him. Jesus is embodied in the sacraments. Jesus is embodied in the lives of the saints. Jesus is embodied in the little ones of the earth. These rich and complex ways of coming to learn Jesus form the next part of our meditation.

CHAPTER 2

Learning Jesus Through Tradition

Jesus is most fully and consistently learned within the context of the believing community of the church, because the risen Lord identifies himself with this community. Jesus is "life-giving Spirit" (1 Cor. 15:45) most directly for those who by their baptism and their "drinking of the Spirit" (1 Cor. 12:13) have entered into the energy field that is Jesus' continuing existence in the world. Jesus promised in Matthew 18:20, "Where two or three are gathered together in my name, I am there among them," and told the disciples in the great commission, "Behold, I am with you always until the close of the age" (Matt. 28:20).

Saul the persecutor sought to extirpate those meeting in Jesus' name (Gal. 1:13). He considered their proclamation of Jesus as risen Lord to be blasphemous. When he was knocked to the ground by a great light, he was asked, "Saul, Saul, why are you persecuting me?" He naturally asked in return, "Who are you, Lord?" and received the clear reply, "I am Jesus whom you are persecuting" (Acts 9:4–5). Similarly, John saw the Son of man standing among the seven candlesticks identified as the seven churches of Asia Minor to which John was writing (Rev. 1:20), and he was told, "I am the First and the Last and the Living One. I was dead and behold I am living forever. And I hold the keys of death and of Hades" (Rev. 1:18).

Jesus is known and loved in the community of faith not as an object of study but as a personal presence and sustaining power. And if the faith community is the place where the living Jesus is most explicitly invoked and encountered, it is also the living repository of knowledge concerning the humanity of Jesus. It must not be forgotten that, apart from the pathetically few fragments of evidence concerning Jesus from Greco-Roman and Jewish sources, everything we know about Jesus' life and ministry before his death comes from the community that also celebrated his continuing and more powerful presence within it as Living One.

The church given birth by the resurrection of Jesus preceded any writings about him. And the texts that speak of Jesus, whether in the form of narratives, visions, or letters, were composed by people who were convinced that one they had known in the flesh was now alive in the Spirit and embodied in their midst. Their memory of his past was selected and shaped by their continuing experience of him in the present. But by no means did that present experience obliterate or falsify that past; rather the church understood that it saw more truly into who Jesus had been because of who he now was. There would be no real knowledge of Jesus available to us today were it not for the church's tradition, which extends from the day of Pentecost down to our own day.

The decision to learn Jesus within the framework of the tradition of the church that celebrates and worships him as the Living One is a choice decisively different from that made by two groups of people today who also proclaim an interest in Jesus but do so in open or covert rejection of the church's tradition. Most obviously, this reliance on tradition distinguishes those who believe in a resurrected Jesus from those seeking a "historical Jesus" behind the Gospel narratives, questers whose fundamental premise is that the church's understanding of Jesus is wrong and in need of correction. Such questers see themselves as the contemporary equivalent of the ancient evangelists, with equal access to information about Jesus and equal authorization—presumably on the basis of their learning and sincerity—to revise the portrayal of Jesus in the Gospels. Their endeavor explicitly opposes the tradition, both as it shaped the memory of Jesus in the beginning and as it proclaims Jesus today.

Respect for the tradition of the church also distinguishes believers in the resurrected Jesus from the entrepreneurial proclaimers of Jesus on television and the lecture circuit who claim for themselves exclusive right to be

24

called authentic Christians, yet whose understanding of Jesus is utterly idiosyncratic and individualistic. If less blatant than the Jesus questers, televangelists also implicitly reject the tradition. They are pure biblicists who treat the New Testament as a divinely inspired text that can be quoted atomistically and at random and who believe that they can bypass any community norms for reading because they are personally called or inspired to preach—which apparently also gives them an inspired capacity to read. The contempt for "organized Christianity" expressed by some Jesus questers is different not in kind, but only in tone, from the arrogant assumption of authority over tradition expressed by televangelistic marketers of Jesus.

An embrace of tradition must be undertaken with an awareness of the risk involved: the willingness to learn Jesus in the context of tradition demands a combination of loyalty and criticism, and either without the other becomes distorted. Loyalty is ideally the premise for true criticism, just as critical awareness is a necessary component of loyalty. Without critical awareness, tradition can become idolatrous, replacing the living Jesus with established formulas about Jesus or ossified interpretations of him. The best sort of critical intelligence insists that the community's loyalty must be directed to the living Lord, not to its own precedents. It is the Lord to whom the tradition is always answerable, not vice versa. But if loyalty without criticism becomes lifeless, so also can criticism without loyalty become mere carping and complaining.

A commitment to the community of believers and to the tradition represents both risk and the loss of a certain autonomy. It therefore ill suits those who consider life to be a matter of careful calculation, cool reason, and individual autonomy. For them, the loss is greater than the gain. But for those who make such a commitment, the situation is reversed: the great gain of learning the living Jesus is worth any other loss. They agree with Paul's position in Philippians 3:7–11:

Whatever gain I had, I counted as loss for the sake of Christ. Indeed I count everything as loss because of the surpassing worth of knowing Christ Jesus my Lord. For his sake I have suffered the loss of all things, and count them as refuse, in order that I might gain Christ and be found in him, not having a righteousness of my own based on law, but that which is through the faith of Christ, the righteousness from God that depends on faith, that I may know him and the power of his resurrection, and may share his sufferings, becoming like him in his death, that if possible I may attain the resurrection from the dead. (RSV, slightly emended)

A Community of Disciples

In the Gospel narratives, Jesus is shown in the midst of a group of people who follow him in a special and more intimate fashion than the crowds. These followers are called disciples *(mathētai),* which in Greek means simply "learners." In each of the Gospels, the disciples are the ones with whom Jesus spends most of his time, to whom he reveals himself most directly, and toward whom he directs his most challenging instructions. During his ministry, the disciples learn from him in a variety of ways: they watch him heal the sick and exorcise those afflicted with demons; they sail with him on calm and stormy waters; they wander the village lanes of Galilee and the streets of Jerusalem; they eat and drink with him in the houses of the pious and the impious; they pray with him on the mountain and see on his face for a moment a glimpse of glory; they follow him to the brink of his arrest and trial but then turn back in fear.

Because the risen Lord Jesus also called a community into being, and through the Holy Spirit was present to the resulting *ekklēsia,* early believers could see themselves in continuity with those disciples who followed Jesus through Galilee in his ministry. The church formed an ongoing community of disciples who encountered Jesus and learned from him together in a variety of ways.

The narratives and visions and letters that speak of Jesus in the New Testament were all written within and for such communities of disciples. The writers of those documents shared the same convictions we have about the presence of Jesus within the church. John's Revelation was written to the seven churches in Asia Minor. The letters of Paul and James and Peter and John were written to churches (or delegates to churches) in Asia Minor and Europe. The Gospels were directed to readers in communities of faith. The compositions written for such communities were in turn read aloud to their members as they were assembled in worship as a way to teach about the meaning of life with God in light of the crucified and raised Messiah Jesus. The authors of the New Testament writings assumed that what they taught was to be learned within such a community of faith.

The same assumption is found among those of us who gather now in the name of Jesus. We are convinced not only that he is "in the midst of us" (Matt. 18:20) but that our lives are defined by his presence to us even more than they are by our presence to each other. As Paul says in Romans 14:7–9:

> None of us lives to himself and none of us dies to himself. If we live, we live to the Lord, and if we die, we die to the Lord; so then, whether we live or whether we die, we are the Lord's. For to this end Christ died and lived again, that he might be Lord both of the dead and of the living. (RSV)

Our learning *of* Jesus and our learning *from* Jesus therefore take place in common. The tradition remains alive precisely because of this process of learning and living in relationship to Jesus within the community.

Since Jesus has identified himself with this community that can be called his "body" (see Rom. 12:4–5; 1 Cor. 6:15; 12:12–27; Eph. 4:12–16;

Col. 1:18), each of its members can influence and help build the body as a whole. Two important corollaries follow. The first is that each one of us can learn from the others in the community of faith. No one member of the community has so much of the truth about Jesus that he has no need to learn. Conversely, no one member of the community has *no* truth about Jesus so that she has no responsibility to teach. The second corollary is as crucial: the community context is one in which discernment can be exercised concerning the teaching and learning of Jesus. The best protection against overactive imagination, the projection of desire, and the manipulation of symbols is the exchange of witness and discernment within the community. The discernment that Paul wants applied to prophecy within the community (1 Cor. 14:26–33) applies also to the learning of Jesus: "Test everything; hold fast to the good, abstain from every form of evil" (1 Thess. 5:21), and "Test the spirits whether they are from God" (1 John 4:1).

The process of witnessing and discerning within the church has gone on from the beginning and has shaped the tradition within which Christians now learn Jesus. Most particularly, the tradition has framed such learning by its discernment concerning the canon of Scripture, the creed, and the teaching authority of the church.

The Canon of Scripture

One of the most decisive moments in Christianity's self-definition was its decision to canonize certain writings and not others. The process of canonization was at first an organic one: communities that had received a letter from an apostle or a narrative concerning Jesus exchanged those documents with other churches; such exchanges led to local collections of texts. The authoritative character of such texts was symbolized by their being read in the context of worship together with the texts of Torah (the law, the prophets, and the writings) that Christians had taken over from the synagogue. By exchanging letters and other writings, Christians were in effect stating an instinct concerning the universal and normative character of those documents: what Paul said to the Corinthians in the past was now also regarded as pertinent to the Ephesians in the present. The historical meaning of the texts was not their only significance, then; through them, God could continue to speak to the church in every age and in every place.

The process was slow, natural, and largely noncontroversial until the middle of the second century. Not every community had precisely the same documents, of course, especially in the beginning. Collections varied in both size and content. Some churches had local favorites, for example, that other communities found of little interest. But by the first decades of the second century, many churches were aware of more than one Gospel, and some had several in their collections. Paul's letters, the Letter to the Hebrews, and the Letter of James were also used in several communities.

The crisis heated up on two fronts in the middle of the second century. From one side (especially from among the Gnostics) there came many new texts that offered an understanding of Jesus and of discipleship quite at odds with that found in Matthew, Mark, Luke, and John. In such writings, Jesus appeared less as a real person than as a heavenly emanation; his significance was to be found less in how he lived and died than in his message of liberation from the body and the world. Discipleship was seen not as following in the path of Jesus' suffering to a future life with God, but as a present celebration of enlightenment given by the knowledge coming from Jesus, the revealer.

From another side there was pressure to reduce the size of the church's collection. Marcion thought that Paul was the only true apostle and considered only his letters—along with a suitably expurgated version of the Gospel of Luke—to be Scripture. Everything else in the New Testament, he thought, was sponsored by the agents of the malevolent God of the Jews. (It goes without saying that Marcion rejected the Old Testament.) Tatian, in turn, considered four divergent Gospels a scandal and harmonized them in his production of the *Diatesseron*, which wove the four versions into one. Both Marcion and Tatian were intensely hostile to the physical world and the world of culture and crafted a Christianity that rejected the world through asceticism.

The pressures of expansion and contraction demanded a decision concerning what compositions were to be read in the church. The traditional canon of the church was forged in this controversial setting. What was at stake was not simply a list of books, but the view of the world, of Jesus, and of Christian life contained in them. The identity of intentional communities is very much formed by the documents that are allowed to shape their discussions. The principle "We are what we read" applied directly to second-century Christians. Was Christianity going to be a public and institutional witness to the humanity of Jesus and the way of the cross and resurrection? Or was it to be an enlightenment movement that saw Jesus as the transmitter of a saving knowledge available only to the elite?

The church settled first on the present writings of the Old Testament. It thus asserted continuity between Israel and the church as well as discontinuity: Jesus must be seen with reference to Torah as well as transcending Torah. The church then included the present twenty-seven compositions in the New Testament canon. By rejecting Marcion and Tatian, the church asserted that it was comfortable with multiple witnesses and interpretations of Jesus. By rejecting the Gnostic writings, it asserted that there were limits to its tolerance for diversity and that it recognized within the variety of New Testament images of Jesus a unity that it could not discern in those other writings.

Since the discovery of the Gnostic library at Nag Hammadi in 1945, some scholars have agitated for a reopening of the canon. It has become popular to characterize the canonizers in unflattering terms, as though their debates were a matter only of narrow political or ideological concern and not the very essence of Christian identity based in the truth about Jesus. Yet the present writings were canonized in large part because they were thought to be the earliest and best witnesses to Jesus and the early church, and nothing in recent discoveries has proven otherwise. Not even the champions of the Coptic *Gospel of Thomas* will argue that as a whole it is earlier than the canonical Gospels.

But not only the antiquity of these writings proved decisive. Much more important was the fact that the Jesus portrayed and witnessed to in the canonical writings corresponded—and corresponds still—to the Jesus experienced in the lives of the faithful. These and not other writings were canonized because of the sense of the church that, read together and as a whole, they accurately (if not exhaustively) witnessed to the truth of Jesus and had the capacity to communicate that truth to every generation and every embodiment of the church.

These documents both enable the realization of Christian identity in the future and secure continuity with Christians in the past. The most fundamental identity decision made by the church in every generation, therefore, is the decision to have these and only these compositions read aloud in the assembly as the Word of God, and to use these and only these compositions as the basis for debate within the community concerning fidelity to God's rule in present circumstances. Any effort to change the canon must be recognized for what it truly is: the desire to change Christian identity. When scholars publish a book called *The Five Gospels* that includes the *Gospel of Thomas* with the four canonical Gospels, the goal of their packaging is patent.

The risk involved in committing oneself to a community that lives within the framework of the traditional canon is clear. How can one ever know that the decisions made in the past were correct? How could one be sure that the image of Jesus in the four canonical Gospels—so obviously different from that in the Gnostic Gospels—is in fact the true image of Jesus? One *cannot* know such things with certainty. This risk requires a trust in God that the community meeting in the name of the resurrected Jesus through all these centuries has not fundamentally been misled. But the risk is, after all, no greater than that involved in believing in the first place that God raised Jesus from the dead, and entrusting one's life to the conviction that Jesus lives now as powerful and present Lord.

It is surely wrong to suggest, however, that entrusting oneself to the tradition in this matter is a form of alienation or intellectual dishonesty. The diversity of the canon is quite considerable enough to enable criticism as well as loyalty. In effect, rather than establishing a univocal version of the gospel, the canon institutionalizes a diversity of witness and interpretation and thereby enables a vigorous and enlivening debate precisely on the basis of these texts. And if the tradition should demand obedience to itself rather than to the living Lord, we do not need to import a recently discovered text from the sands of Egypt to challenge such presumption. We can find a sufficient counter to any absolutizing claim within the canon itself. More than that: the canon of Scripture is only one of the elements in the framework for learning Jesus within the community of faith. And all these elements are themselves relativized by the overwhelming reality of the living Lord, who continues to surprise.

The Creed

The second critical element in Christian self-definition is the creed—or, as it was first designated, the "rule of faith." The word *rule (kanōn)* is exactly the same as the one translated as "canon." That etymological correspondence confirms that the mid-second-century debate over which books to read in the church was also, as I have suggested, a conflict over the identity of Jesus and of discipleship. Just as the church needed to establish a collection of those early witnesses that testified reliably to the truth that is in Jesus, so did it need to articulate its sense of how those witnesses should be heard.

These conflicts happened so long ago that they now seem remote. It is easy today for scholars to scoff at the creed as a form of "theological tyranny" obscuring the real, historical Jesus—as though there had been no real urgency to shaping the rule of faith (apart from the desire of bishops for control). The reality is otherwise. The crisis was both severe and fundamental. It was severe because the orthodox party that finally prevailed was by no means necessarily always the more powerful or numerous party; for several centuries entire parts of the Mediterranean world were dominated by alternative versions of Christianity. The outcome was genuinely in doubt, especially since the battle had to be waged entirely by means of intellectual instruments. Neither orthodoxy nor heterodoxy had the political means to establish itself. (Constantine was still more than 150 years in the future.)

The crisis was also fundamental. If Marcion was correct, for example, then there was not one God who was both the creator and savior of humanity, but two separate and opposed Gods: one who mischievously created the world and the other who rescued humans from its fleshly imprisonment. In such a scheme, the God of the Old Testament is the evil creator. Jesus reveals and represents an alien God who has nothing to do with creation and whose only business is salvation. Marcion's "modification" of the gospel was in reality a complete recasting of it. Marcion's alternative rule of faith led to a rereading even of the canonical Scriptures. In 2 Corinthians 4:4, for example, Paul says, "In their case [namely, the unbelievers] the god of this world has blinded the minds of the unbelievers, to keep them from seeing the light of the gospel of the glory of Christ who is the likeness of God" (rsv). Marcion read "god of this world" as a literal reference to a creator God who opposed the God of Jesus. The orthodox creed, in contrast, begins, "We believe in one God, the Father almighty, Maker of Heaven and Earth . . . and in Jesus Christ his Son our Lord." The statement of belief in "one God" who both creates and saves is a *defining* statement over against readings of the text that distort the reality experienced by the community. It expresses a sense of the overall point of Scripture that guides the reading of specific passages consonant with that overall construal. Thus, although it is recognized that Paul's reference to

33

"the god of this world" is indeed difficult and obscure—and in fact *could* be read the way Marcion read it—within the framework of this community's code of reading it is not taken as scriptural proof that there are in reality two gods.

As a fully formed set of propositions, the creed was shaped in response to conflict over the nature of Christian identity, just as the canon was settled because of dispute over authoritative writings. And just as the process of canon formation preceded the crisis as a natural instinct of sharing the witnesses to Jesus among communities, so also did the creed begin its development as a natural expression of convictions about God's work in Jesus.

The roots of the declaration, "We believe in one God," go all the way back to Israel's distinctive declaration, "Hear, O Israel: The Lord our God is one Lord" (Deut. 6:4). The conviction is given explicit voice also by Paul when he says, "God is one" (Rom. 3:30). Yet as early as Paul also, the community's experience of the risen and living Jesus was so powerful as to demand some propositional expression of who Jesus must be in order to have altered reality so fundamentally. The earliest of such confessions may well have been "Jesus is Lord" (see 1 Cor. 12:3; Rom. 10:9; Phil. 2:11; Acts 2:36). This simple yet powerful confession bears within itself implicitly all the later creedal development, for it poses the question of what it means to call both the God of Israel and Jesus of Nazareth "Lord." To recognize in the risen Jesus one who now lives with God's own life demands some expression of how Jesus is related both to the source of all reality and to the rest of creation.

Paul shows us an early effort at such articulation in 1 Corinthians 8:4–8:

> We know that "an idol has no real existence" and that "there is no God but one." For although there may be many so-called gods in

heaven or on earth—as indeed there are many "gods" and many "lords" yet for us there is one God, the Father, from whom are all things and for whom we exist, and one Lord, Jesus Christ, through whom are all things and through whom we exist. (RSV)

This is an altogether remarkable statement, containing in itself the germ of later creedal development. Notice how in this text, written within twenty-five years of Jesus' death, the experience of him as the life-giving Spirit in the community enables him to be confessed as God's agent in creation as well as God's agent in the re-creation of humans. Also noteworthy is Paul's tiny phrase "for us." The creed never loses its character as an expression of the experience and commitment of real persons. As a confession of the community's belief, the creed both "believes" more than each member of the community and falls short of the richness of faith in the life of each member of the community. It is not an adequate expression, but it is a true witness.

The propositions of the creed reveal how the continuing experience of the living Lord in the faith community led to a more developed sense of who and what Jesus truly is: the Son of God whom God sent in the fullness of time so that humans might receive adoption as God's children (Gal. 4:4–5). The creed gives concrete expression to the church's "learning" of Jesus. It is not by review of the historical record but above all by the continuing experience of Jesus' transforming presence and power in the Spirit that the church comes to understand that Jesus is "God from God, Light from Light, true God from true God, begotten not made, one in being with the Father, through whom all things are made"; for, with Paul, the church progressively came to understand that beneath and within the particulars of an individual life, "God was in Christ reconciling the world to himself" (2 Cor. 5:19).

But does the creed that gives such explicit expression to the divinity of

35

Christ also depreciate his humanity? This is the implication behind the charge that the creed has imposed a "theological tyranny" on the Jesus of history. Are "creedal Christians" alienated from the living Jesus?

The charge misunderstands the function of the creed. The rule of faith is not the same thing as the living response of faith. Rather, it is the community's public expression of the framework of belief within which it carries out its life. The creed is to living faith as the rulebook is to the game of baseball; the rules set the necessary frame, but within that frame the most astonishing variety of things can happen with bat and ball. Likewise, the believer's response to the living Jesus is something much richer and various than the propositions of the rule of faith.

Furthermore, the widely used Nicene-Constantinople Creed pays explicit attention to the humanity of Jesus. Jesus is said to have been "conceived by the Holy Spirit" and "born of the virgin Mary"; he "suffered under Pontius Pilate, [was] crucified, died and was buried." Birth of a specific woman and death at the decree of a certain identifiable Roman official of the first century are details that distinguish Jesus from any cosmic myth as well as from any other human ever born. But perhaps I am being too literal. Perhaps the real objection is that creedal Christians think of Jesus' humanity only in abstract terms, without appreciating its importance; perhaps they have allowed his divinity to swallow up his humanity.

But has this been the case within the tradition? The evidence does not suggest it. The same patristic theologians who exalted the divinity of Christ and spun such fine metaphysical distinctions concerning "nature" and "person" also preached sermons on the Gospels that meditated in detail on the humanity of Jesus. And if the Middle Ages were the high point of abstract, propositional theology, they were also a time when Jesus' humanity was a constant subject of prayer, meditation, music, and art. The frescoes of Giotto, for example, were not painted by someone neglectful of the humanity of Jesus.

The creed provides a framework for the learning of Jesus within the community because it maintains the tension between two equally powerful convictions concerning Jesus. The first is that a human person who was born like us and who died as we must also die continues to encounter us in our specific humanity. The second is that when we are touched by Jesus, we are also touched by God.

The Teaching Authority of the Church

The commitment to learn the living Jesus within the context of the church's tradition means coming to grips also with the leaders who from the beginning have been entrusted in a special way with maintaining that tradition. It is this aspect of tradition—namely, its explicitly institutional character—that both the scholarly questers after the historical Jesus and the televangelistic marketers of Jesus most despise. Academics resist authority in the name of intellectual freedom and integrity; freelance preachers reject ecclesial authority in the name of charismatic freedom and power.

Those who commit themselves to tradition can scarcely miss the same inadequacies of human leadership that have been so brilliantly and consistently displayed in the history of Christianity. They know that ministers of the gospel are often not as holy as they should be, are seldom as intelligent as we would like them to be, and all too often identify the tradition with their own self-interest. No matter how egalitarian the leadership of a community, or how hierarchical, the same human frailty and pettiness appear.

Yet there can scarcely be tradition without institutional leadership. Christianity is not simply a loose assemblage of those who at any time prefer to associate with each other; it is a people with a history and a mission that must be articulated in specific social arrangements and dynamics. The witness of leaders in the community, furthermore, is at the heart of this tradition itself. Those commissioned by the risen Lord as apostles were the first in a long line of shepherds for this flock. If every pope and bishop and presbyter and pastor and preacher has been unequal to the task, that inadequacy has not made their role of maintaining the living thread of tradition any less essential.

The teaching authority remains essential today, however difficult it is to reconcile with the egalitarian and anti-establishment urges of our age. No more than the canon or the creed can the leadership of the church arrogate to itself the loyalty that is owed only to the living Lord; no more than the canon or the creed does this leadership adequately express the meaning of the tradition, much less the Lord in whose name the tradition exists. The teaching authority of the community functions best when it is not isolated. The teaching office of the church requires the voice of prophecy to be alive if it is not to grow distended: through prophets the living Jesus can speak in new ways. And the preservers of tradition need also to hear the voices of theologians whose task is not so much to preserve as it is to extend the boundaries of our understanding of the mystery of Christ. The tradition is impoverished if the voice of prophecy is stilled and if the teaching of theologians is, for whatever reason, made an enemy rather than an enricher of the tradition.

Like the canon and the creed, the teaching authority of leaders helps provide a framework for learning Jesus in the community. From generation to generation from the beginning, hands have reached out to select, hands have been laid on heads, words of commission have been whispered in the ears of those whose mission is defined by the task of preserving and protecting the tradition within which Jesus can continue to be learned.

CHAPTER 3

He Bodies Forth Whose Glory Is Past Change

When I speak of learning Jesus within the framework of the church's tradition, I by no means intend to imply that Jesus is contained or even adequately expressed by the canon, creed, or teaching authority of the believing community. The experience of Saul the persecutor emphatically demonstrates the opposite: the living Lord Jesus can operate outside that frame, can in fact shake or shatter that frame with his presence.

Likewise, when I refer to the church as the resurrected Lord's body—a metaphor offered, as we saw in the previous chapter, in the New Testament—I am not suggesting that Jesus' capacity to embody his presence is controlled by any human power. That metaphor simply communicates that for reasons unknown to us, the risen Lord has chosen this inadequate, frail, and all too often fallible body as his most visible and sustained mode of presence in the world. The Lord's sovereign freedom determines the relationship, not the church. The mystical body of the church is less a container than a sign that points beyond itself to the life it so inadequately expresses.

The church does not—or at least should not—claim to express the presence of Jesus fully; rather, the church should witness to the ways in which the power of the Resurrected One transcends and is manifested outside its bounds. But since the power and life of the risen Lord do vivify the communal body, the church is something more than a simple sign. It is a symbol that shares in the reality toward which it points. It is, to play on the wonderful phrase of Edward Schillebeeckx, the primordial sacrament of encounter with Christ.

The witness of the church to the resurrected Jesus is embodied in at least three ways: in the worship life of the community (above all, in the sacrament of the eucharist), in the lives of the saints, and in the little ones of the earth——those of whom the church mostly consists and whom it is above all called to serve and to embrace. In these embodiments the living Jesus continues to shape, to challenge, and to teach the world.

Learning Jesus in Worship

From the beginning, Christians have taken the promise of Jesus in Matthew 18:20 to be realized in their experience: "Where two or three are gathered in my name, I am there in the midst of them." The Letter of James testifies to the conviction that the risen Lord's continuing presence in the community can heal the sick: when elders are convoked by an ill brother or sister, and that person is anointed with oil "in the name of the Lord," the prayer of faith can save the sick person and "the Lord will raise him up" (James 5:14–15). Paul also twice lists "gifts of healing" that are given by the Spirit within the body of Christ (1 Cor. 12:9, 30).

Such "signs and wonders" can be accomplished among the faithful (see also 2 Cor. 12:12; Gal. 3:5) because the name in which they gather is that of the living Lord who has triumphed over death itself and works among them through the Holy Spirit he supplies (see Phil. 1:19; Gal. 3:5). The gestures of healing demonstrate how through the prayers and bodily gestures of the community, the power of the Resurrected One "takes body" through the work of the Spirit and extends itself through the bodies of those touched by this power.

The reality expressed in crisis through acts of healing is enacted by the church regularly through the sacrament of the eucharist. This is the supreme example of the way in which the glorious body of the risen Lord both transcends and is immanent within the body of the believing community. From the beginning, believers have "recognized him" in the gestures of breaking and blessing (Luke 24:31), and he was made "known to them in the breaking of the bread" (Luke 24:35).

The classic Christian conviction that in the elements of bread and wine in the Lord's Supper the body of the Lord Jesus is made "really" or "sacramentally" present through the power of his Holy Spirit invoked by the prayer of the community—even when this conviction has been distorted by obsessive preoccupation with the manner in which this might occur—is the church's most consistent ritual witness to the reality of the resurrection. When the words Jesus spoke at his last meal over bread and wine are pronounced by the church in memory of him, his "death is announced until he comes" (1 Cor. 11:23–26). The words do not simply remember a dead teacher; they express the presence and await the return of the Living One.

When Paul reminds the Corinthians of this truth that he handed on to them and that he himself "received from the Lord" (1 Cor. 11:23), he connects the presence of the Living One at the meal to the life of the community in two other important ways. First, Paul insists that eating and drinking the bread and wine at the table of the Lord is truly "a sharing in the body of the Messiah, because we who are many are one bread, one body, for we all share in the one bread" (10:16–17). Just as sharing in idol worship involves the participants in spiritual entanglements that are destructive—"I do not want you to become sharers with demons" (10:20)—even more so those who share in the bread and cup of the risen Jesus "drink the one Spirit" and become the body of the Messiah (see 1 Cor. 12:13).

Second, Paul demands that the church understand the link between its members and Jesus in terms of consistent moral behavior. If wealthier and more powerful members at the meal eat and drink while others go hungry, then the "assembly of God" (11:22) has been despised. The very attitude that has "shamed those who have nothing" (11:22) is tantamount to "not discerning the body" (11:28). "Therefore my brothers and sisters," says Paul to the Corinthians, "when you have come together to eat, receive each other" (11:33). To the Romans he says, "Therefore welcome one another just as Christ has welcomed you unto the glory of God" (Rom. 15:7). Paul demonstrates how the eucharistic presence of the risen Jesus is itself a way the community learns from Jesus what it means to be the body of Christ.

The worship life of the church also enables Christians to learn of and from Jesus through the reading of Scripture and preaching, and through prophecy and prayer.

Within the liturgical assembly, the reading of Gospels and Epistles that speak explicitly about Jesus accompanies the reading of passages from the Old Testament and the responsorial singing of the Psalms. Especially when the lectionary is used, Gospel passages containing a segment of a narrative about Jesus are thus given new and complex contexts made up of narratives and prophecies and writings addressed first of all to Israel and, in the case of the Psalms, also prayed by Israel. Those who hear these texts are invited to construct, in an almost kaleidoscopic fashion, an image of Jesus with many different and changing dimensions. The ways in which the Jesus story echoes or answers the texts of Torah; the ways in which the words of the Psalms can be sung as the words of Jesus as well as the words of Israel and the words of the church; the ways in which the Epistles set up angles of intersection and tangent with the story of Jesus; the ways in which all of these intertextual signals interact with the living experience of Jesus in the lives of the listeners—all this rich complexity creates a sense of Jesus within the imagination of the listeners that escapes literal or univocal delineation.

No less complex are the ways in which the words of scriptural texts are brought into new combinations and given new dimensions by the words spoken in worship—not only in the eucharistic prayer of thanksgiving and the community prayers of petition, but also in the speech of the community that prays now with the words of the blind men by the road, "Lord have mercy" (Matt. 20:30), and now with the words of the prophet Isaiah, "Holy, Holy, Holy, Lord God of Hosts" (Isa. 6:3), and now with David the Psalmist and the people of Jerusalem, "Blessed is he who comes in the name of the Lord" (Mark 11:9; Ps. 118:26), and now with the words taught the disciples by Jesus, "Our Father" (Matt. 6:9), and now with the words of John the Baptist, "Lamb of God who takes away the sin of the world" (John 1:29), and finally with the words of the centurion, "Lord, I am not worthy that you should come under my roof, but speak the word and your servant shall be healed" (Luke 7:7).

Preaching in the liturgical assembly further actualizes these texts by connecting them explicitly to the experience and situation of the church in particular circumstances. The understanding of Jesus is deepened and given new dimensions by the ways in which the stories from the past and the stories of the present are brought into conversation. Those who read the texts and those who speak about the texts bear witness to the reality of Jesus as anticipated in the law and the prophets of Torah, as both song and singer of the Psalms, and as the one who heals and reconciles in the hills of Galilee, in the churches of James and Peter and Paul, and in the storefront assemblies and grand cathedrals and detoxification centers of today.

From the beginning, the Spirit poured out on the faithful by the resurrected Jesus was understood as the spirit of prophecy (Acts 2:16–33). The presence of this spirit of prophecy was a powerful sign of the presence of the Living One among those who gathered in his name. As we read in Acts 4:29–31:

> "And now Lord, look upon their threats and grant to thy servants to speak thy word with all boldness, while thou stretchest out thy hand to heal, and signs and wonders are performed through the name of thy Holy Servant Jesus." And when they had prayed, the place in which they were gathered together was shaken; and they were all filled with the Holy Spirit and spoke the word of God with boldness. (RSV)

In Paul's churches, prophets spoke in the assembly through the Holy Spirit (1 Cor. 12:10, 29), and through their words listeners were convicted, were called to account, had their secrets disclosed, and recognized that God was at work in the assembly (1 Cor. 14:24–25). In such fashion, prophecy built up the church (14:5). Such spiritual utterances needed to be discerned by all (12:10; 14:29), but the voice of prophecy was not to be suppressed: "Do not suppress the Spirit, do not despise prophesying, but test everything" (1 Thess. 5:19–20). Through the Holy Spirit's prophetic voice within the community, the church came to a deeper awareness of the meaning of Scripture (see Acts 2:14–36; 8:26–40; 15:12–29; John 11:16; 2 Pet. 1:16–21) and Jesus' own words (see Acts 11:15–18; John 16:7–15).

Perhaps the most dramatic example is the Book of Revelation, in which we find stated, "The spirit of prophecy is the witness of Jesus" (Rev. 19:10). The entire composition consists of "words of prophecy" (1:2) that come from the Risen One—he who died and who now lives forever (1:18), and who through this prophecy addresses the churches of Asia (Rev. 2:1–3:22). The Book of Revelation demonstrates the understanding of Christian prophecy as a continuation of the living voice of Jesus within the church, and in its reshaping of the symbols of Torah around the figure of Jesus—the "lamb who was slain" (5:6) but who, as the Living One, remains the "faithful witness" (1:5)—it also shows how such prophecy enables the church to learn Jesus in new ways.

As the spirit of prophecy continues in the church, calling it to renewed fidelity and challenging it with new understanding, so also Christians continue to learn Jesus through the experience of prayer. Some of this learning is mediated through the prayer spoken in the assembly, as when Paul addresses Jesus, "*Maranatha:* Our Lord, come" (1 Cor. 16:22); or when Peter seeks guidance for the replacement of Judas, "You, Lord, know the hearts of all. Show which one of these two you have chosen to take the place in this service and apostleship" (Acts 1:24–25); or when the elders in the vision of Revelation sing, "Worthy art thou to take the scroll and open its seals, for thou wast slain, and by thy blood didst ransom men for God from every tribe and tongue and people and nation, and hast made them a kingdom and priests to our God, and they shall reign on earth" (Rev. 5:9–10, RSV).

But Jesus is encountered also in prayer that is not mediated ritually, in states of vision and ecstasy. Paul's encounter with the risen Lord on the way to Damascus (Acts 9:1–9), enabled him to say, "Have I not seen the Lord Jesus?" (1 Cor. 9:1). He learned from that encounter how "the God who said, 'Let light shine out of darkness,' has shone in our hearts to illuminate the knowledge of God's glory in the face of Christ" (2 Cor. 4:6). Stephen stood in prayer before his accusers as they were about to stone him, crying, "Lord Jesus, receive my Spirit" (Acts 7:39), perhaps learning to die in the same way Jesus himself had (see Luke 23:46) because of the vision preceding his prayer: "Behold, I see the heavens opened and the Son of man standing at the right hand of God" (Acts 7:56). The Lord Jesus also spoke to Paul one night in a vision: "Do not be afraid, but speak and do not be silent, for I am with you and no one shall attack you to harm you. For I have many people in this city" (Acts 18:9). So also Paul described an experience of prayer in the temple: "I was praying in the temple and I went into a trance, and saw him saying to me, 'Hurry and leave Jerusalem quickly because they will not accept your testimony about me'" (Acts 22:17–18).

Sometimes in such visions, more often in the quiet prayer of silence or in meditation on the mysteries of Jesus' ministry, death, and resurrection, Christians through the ages have continued to learn of Jesus by learning *from* Jesus, have come to deeper insights into his identity and a more secure grasp of the meaning of following in his path. Through such prayer, and with the help of the Holy Spirit, Jesus has been able to shape men and women according to his image, fashioning for himself another embodiment in the lives of the saints.

Learning Jesus in the Saints

The most compelling and convincing evidence of the resurrection is the existence of Christian saints. The Spirit poured out on believers by the resurrected Jesus is not only a spirit of prophecy directing their speech (Acts 2:14–21); it is also a spirit of holiness (Rom. 1:4) directing and transforming their lives according to the image of Jesus (Rom. 8:29). Paul's language is most dramatic:

Now the Lord is the Spirit. And where the Spirit of the Lord is, there is freedom. And we all, gazing on the glory of the Lord with unveiled face, are being transformed into the same image from glory to glory, just as from the Lord who is Spirit. (2 Cor. 3:17–18)

If Christians "live by the Spirit" that comes from Jesus, then they are also to "walk by the Spirit" (Gal. 5:25), which Paul explicates as "fulfilling the law of Christ" by bearing one another's burdens (Gal. 6:2). The pattern of Jesus' character—the way he "loved me and gave himself for me" (Gal. 2:20b)—is now to be the pattern of the Christian's life, for like Paul we "have been crucified with Christ; it is no longer I who live but Christ who lives in me; and the life I now live in the flesh I live by the faith of the Son of God" (Gal. 2:20a). Paul speaks of "putting on the Lord Jesus" (Rom. 13:14) and of "putting on the new person which is being renewed in knowledge after the image of its creator . . . Christ [who] is all in all" (Col. 3:10–11).

The idea of imitating moral exemplars is as old as human wisdom. What is distinctive to Christian conviction is that both the pattern and the power to follow it are given to humans by the living Lord Jesus through the Holy Spirit. The process of sanctification to which Christians are called (1 Thess. 4:3; 1 Cor. 1:2) is a process of growing in conformity to the "mind of Christ" (1 Cor. 2:16)—a process that results in a life that is, in reality, a continuing embodiment of Jesus' own: "Present your bodies as a living sacrifice, holy and acceptable to God, which is your spiritual worship. Do not be conformed to this world but be transformed by the renewal of your mind, that you may test what is the will of God, what is good and acceptable and perfect" (Rom. 12:1–2, RSV).

This path of holiness does not consist in an imitation of the historical incidentals of Jesus' human life; these remain in the past and are irrecoverable. Jesus' specific time and place in the world, his maleness and Jewishness, his speech patterns and his deeds, his mode of ministry and his manner at meals, even his enemies and his way of fighting them: all these help define the Jesus of the past but no longer define the Jesus of the present, who finds specific bodily expression in the lives of others through the power of the resurrection.

Paul and Peter and the anonymous author of Hebrews all grasped that it was the pattern of the Messiah's humanity—his character, as it were—that Christians were called to imitate and were empowered to imitate through the Holy Spirit. The mystery of "incorporation" into Christ meant that one was a "new creation" (2 Cor. 5:17) in which the Spirit of Jesus could direct one's life—in circumstances utterly different from those of Jesus in the past—through the same process of self-giving service, radical obedience, suffering, and new life exemplified by Jesus himself:

> I count everything as loss because of the surpassing worth of knowing Christ Jesus my Lord. For his sake I have suffered the loss of all things and consider them as refuse, in order that I may gain Christ, and *be found in him,* not having a righteousness of my own based on law, but that which is through the faith of Christ, the righteousness from God that is based on faith, *that I may know him and the power of his resurrection, and may share his sufferings, becoming like him in his death, that if possible I may attain the resurrection from the dead.* . . . We await a Savior, the Lord Jesus Christ, who will *change our lowly body to be like his glorious body by the power that enables him to subject all things to himself.* (Phil. 3:8–11, 21, italics added)

To be transformed according to the image of Christ means, therefore, to live by the "mind of Christ" and the "pattern of the Messiah."

It is precisely in this connection that the humanity of Jesus appears as most important in our earliest Christian texts. The transformative work of the Spirit is to replicate in human freedom the character of Jesus. Witness to the reality of God in the face of idolatrous pretense continues the witness borne by Jesus (Rev. 19:10; 1 Tim. 6:11–16). Bearing persecution and social ostracism with faith means that we "go outside the camp bearing the abuse he endured" (Heb. 13:13). Suffering without reviling or complaint requires that we "follow in his steps" (1 Pet. 2:21). Forgiveness of others is to be done "as the Lord has forgiven you" (Col. 3:13; Eph. 4:32). Walking in love is to act "as Christ loved us and handed himself over for us" (Eph. 5:2). Avoiding every kind of vice follows from "learning Christ . . . if indeed you have heard about him and were taught him just as the truth is in Jesus" (Eph. 4:20–21). Welcoming others in the community is to be done "as Christ welcomed you" (Rom. 15:7). Looking to others' interests rather than our own has this basis: "Christ did not please himself" (Rom. 15:3; see Phil. 2:1–11). Relativizing our rights out of concern for others lest our freedom cause them to stumble demands that we have consideration for "the brother for whom Christ died" (1 Cor. 8:11).

From the beginning, Christians have shared the conviction that they were "called to be saints" (Rom. 1:7; 1 Cor. 1:2), to move through this transformation into the image of Jesus through the power of the Holy Spirit that came from Jesus himself as risen Lord. Furthermore, they have believed that this transformation means enacting, in the circumstances specific to their own lives, the same pattern of obediential faith in God and self-giving service to others that was demonstrated by Jesus, so that as he moved through suffering to glory, so also—through participation in his Spirit—would they progress.

From the beginning, Christians have shared the conviction that "the grace of our Lord Jesus Christ" by which they are saved (Acts 15:11; Rom. 5:15; Eph. 2:5) is more than simply a "favor" done them by God; rather, it is in some real sense a "gift" that enables them to share the very life of God through the Spirit that comes to them from Jesus. This gift, furthermore, is not simply potential but actual: "Hope is not shamed, because God's love has been poured into our hearts through the Holy Spirit that has been given to us" (Rom. 5:5). The process of transformation in holiness, therefore, is taking place within human freedom as it opens itself to the freedom given by the Spirit of the Lord (2 Cor 3:17–18).

The understanding within the tradition that there are "saints" in whom the pattern of Jesus the Messiah and Lord can be discerned with particular clarity is an acknowledgment of the reality of grace and a willingness to give glory to God—that is, to recognize the presence and power of God at work in the world. That understanding was an early element in Christian consciousness. Already in Ignatius of Antioch we find a disciple who faced martyrdom with the clear understanding that this path of witnessing to God unto death was a literal following in the way of Jesus. And those friends of Polycarp, bishop of Smyrna, who reported his death at the hands of the authorities also showed in their rendering of his martyrdom that they understood it to be an imitation of Jesus' loving sacrifice for others in obedience to God.

The heart of the Christian tradition is in fact the living succession of holy persons who have been transformed by the Holy Spirit of Jesus. Tradition is not simply the transmission of facts and norms; it is above all the communication of life and identity. And it is through the saints—those who have been transformed by the power of the resurrected Jesus—that the tradition has been enlivened. Some saints have been public figures within the church or within society; their example has been seen by all, their influence obvious. Other saints have been virtually anonymous, known only to a few (and some perhaps only to God); their example and influence are more subtle, though no less real.

It is entirely appropriate for Christians to pay attention to those humans in whom divine transformation is most visibly present, for in the lives of such saints we learn Jesus. We recognize them as saints in the first place because they "show us the Christ": we can see in the pattern of their behavior and in their character the Spirit of Jesus embodied and active in the world. There can be no sanctity unless there be an integrity of word and action such as we see in the Gospel accounts of Jesus; unless there be the

freedom from corruption and double-mindedness such as we find exemplified in Jesus; unless there be a pattern of love and service even to death
such as we find in the actions of Jesus; unless there be wisdom given to others through their foolishness, strength given to others through their weakness, healing given to others through their wounds, enrichment of others
given through their poverty, life given to others through their death.

At the same time, we learn from such saints the multiple ways in
which the mind of Christ can be embodied in the world. We learn that it
can find embodiment in contemplatives and mystics as well as in martyrs.
We discover that it can be found in a life of engagement with the world and
the structures of society, both in the corridors of power and in the alleyways
of raw human need. And in each individual expression of sanctity in which
the mind of Christ is embodied through the freedom of another person, we
"learn Jesus," discovering new dimensions and possibilities of life with the
one we now call Lord. In each of them, we gain "the knowledge of God's
glory on the face of Christ" (2 Cor. 4:6), for what we seek in them is precisely the working of Jesus' transformative Spirit (2 Cor. 3:17–18).

Often enough, the church is surprised by what it learns of Jesus—no,
learns *from* Jesus—through the lives of the saints. Although hagiography
tends to diminish the innovative and sometimes shocking character of the
witness of individual saints, it is important to recognize that the saints are,
in effect, the living voice of prophecy within the church. From Ignatius
of Antioch to Mother Teresa, those most fully suffused with the Spirit of
Jesus and most fully enacting the pattern of Jesus in their lives have also
most emphatically challenged and threatened the assumption that life in
Christ is compatible with a life of comfort and personal or institutional
self-aggrandizement. It is when the mind of Christ is clearly embodied in
the life of an individual *and* when that person challenges the accepted practices and procedures of the community that the church must pay attention,
knowing that it is being called to account by the risen Lord.

It is, indeed, through the signs of holiness in others that each one of us learns Jesus in the first place. Each of us could recite our own "litany of saints" that would include all the people from whom we learned the meaning of life in Christ. The first in my own litany is Bernice Johnson, who as a widowed mother of six children persevered in the faith and prayed under her breath as she moved through her day, "Lord Jesus Christ, have mercy on me a sinner." She spent herself for her children in selfless devotion and thus taught them Jesus; she opened her home for the church of God and for the unlovely and unacceptable and thus taught her children Jesus; she made no discrimination in her friendship and thus taught her children Jesus; she shared what little she possessed with those who had less and thus taught her children Jesus; she suffered every sort of loss with utter confidence in the living God and thus taught her children Jesus. My litany of saints includes others; citing only those who have already gone to join Jesus in glory, I mention Lucy Johnson, David Melancon, Pius Lartigue, Andrew Becnel, Polycarp Sherwood. From being with each of them, from observation of their lives, I learned about Jesus and, I am convinced, I learned from Jesus.

Learning Jesus in the Little Ones of the Earth

The saints are those who serve the needs of the world's poor and outcast, the little ones who have no power of their own. But the saints are also those who know that they receive even more from these little ones than they give, for in the rejected and oppressed of the earth Jesus is especially to be encountered. No great subtlety is required to identify the little ones. In Mark 9:36–37, we read, "And he took a child and put him in their midst; and taking him in his arms, he said to them, 'Whoever receives one among such children in my name receives me; and whoever receives me, receives not me but him who sent me.'"

The child perfectly represents all the world's little ones, not merely because of stature, but because the child signifies everything that a world based on the denial of God wishes to exclude. Children are powerless, needy, intrusive, demanding, fragile, expensive, and care-intensive. Children threaten any sense of a "kingdom" consisting exclusively of the rich and the powerful and the self-sufficient. The dominion of God announced by Jesus has a different standard:

> They were bringing children to him that he might touch them. But the disciples rebuked them. And when Jesus saw it he was indignant and said to them, "Let the children come to me. Do not hinder them; for the rule of God is of such as these. Truly I say to you, whoever does not receive the dominion of God as if it were a child shall not enter it." And he took them in his arms and blessed them, laying his hands upon them. (Mark 10:13–16)

I have translated Mark's version of this story as literally as possible, for the point of Jesus' last statement is different here than in the parallel saying in Matthew 18:3. Matthew, who uses the wording "Unless you turn and become like children, you will never enter the kingdom of heaven," is making the point that we must become childlike. Mark's point, on the other hand, is that the way we receive a child, welcome a child, is the measure of our reception of God's rule! Not to welcome a child—and by extension any of the world's lowly and outcast—is in effect to reject Jesus himself.

Though Matthew chooses another focus in 18:3, this same point is found elsewhere in his Gospel, perhaps even more dramatically. In Matthew 25:31–46, we learn that the judgment levied on the disciples by the Son of man when he comes in his glory will be determined by their behavior toward all the hungry—did they give them food?—and all the thirsty—did they give them drink?—and all the strangers—did they welcome them?—and all the naked—did they clothe them?—and all the sick—did they visit them?—and all those imprisoned—did they come to them? The Son of man explicitly identifies himself with these: "Truly I say to you, as you did it to the least of these my brothers, you did it to me" (25:40, 42).

In the Gospels, Jesus identifies himself with those who are weak and in need, just as he does with the disciples themselves: "Truly I tell you, whoever gives you to drink a cup of water to drink because you bear the name of Christ will by no means lose his reward" (Mark 9:41). Are we to suppose that the resurrected Jesus is any less to be found among the world's little ones?

Precisely the conviction that Jesus does so identify himself lies behind Paul's concern that his communities show special care for the weak, the lowly, the poor, and even the morally inept among them. These are the brothers and sisters "for whom Christ died" (1 Cor. 8:11): "Thus, by sinning against your brethren and wounding their conscience that is weak, *you sin against Christ*" (1 Cor. 8:12, italics added; see also Rom. 14: 20–22). These are the ones who "have nothing" and are "shamed" when others eat to excess at the Lord's Supper while they go hungry, behavior Paul equates, as we saw earlier in the chapter, with "despising the church of God" (1 Cor. 11:22) and failing to "discern the body" of Christ (11:29). These are the ones whose financial support by means of the collection will glorify God by their "obedience in acknowledging the Gospel of Christ" (2 Cor. 9:13). These are the ones who have trespassed and whose correction "in a spirit of compassion" is undertaken with the knowledge that those who do the correcting—whose willingness to bear another's burdens "fulfill[s] the law of Christ" (Gal. 6:2)—are also tempted and can fall.

The same conviction is found in John's insistence that the community of Jesus must live not according to the logic of envy that leads to murder (1 John 3:11–12) but according to the logic of the love shown by Jesus: "In this we have come to know love, that he laid down his life for us. And we ought to lay down our lives for the brothers" (3:16). This love, however, cannot be merely verbal; it must be expressed in action as well: "But if anyone has the world's goods and sees his brother in need yet closes his heart against him, how does God's love abide in him? Little children, let us not love in word and speech but in deed and truth" (1 John 3:17–18, RSV).

James is equally clear in his insistence that faith and love must be spelled out in consistent practices toward those who are among the little ones. It is the depriving of the wages of the poor that cries out to God for justice (James 5:1–6). It is the flattery of the rich person in ostentatious jewelry and the shaming of the poor person in shabby clothes that convict a community of failing to live by "the faith of our Lord Jesus Christ" (2:1). Though God has chosen the poor to be heirs of God's rule, those in the convicted community "despise the poor" (2:5–6). Thus love of neighbor must be spelled out by practical care for the needy: "If a brother or sister is ill-clad and in lack of daily food, and one of you says to them, 'Go in peace, be warmed and filled,' *without giving them the things needed for the body,* what use is it?" (James 2:15–16, italics added).

Peter tells his readers, "In your hearts, sanctify Christ as the Lord" (1 Pet. 3:15). The belief that in the neighbor and in the stranger alike Jesus is to be found and to be served is central to the Christian understanding of sanctity. It is the conviction animating the *Rule of Benedict* in its instructions concerning the sick members of the community: "Before all things and above all things care must be taken of the sick, so that they may be served in very deed as Christ himself; for he said, 'I was sick and ye visited me,' and 'what ye did to one of the least ones, ye did unto me'" (chap. 36). Likewise, concerning guests to the community: "Let all guests that come be received as Christ, for he will say, 'I was a stranger and you took me in.'" Describing the humility to be exercised in the reception of all guests, Benedict says, "Let the head be bowed or the whole body prostrated on the ground, and *so let Christ be worshipped in them, for indeed he is received in their persons.*" And he adds, "In the reception of poor men and pilgrims, special attention should be shown, because *in them Christ is more truly welcomed,* for the fear which the rich inspire is enough of itself to secure them honor" (chap. 53, italics added).

The *Rule of Benedict* is not an idiosyncratic but a classic expression of the operative Christian premise that every person encountered offers, in a very real sense, an encounter with Jesus, and that especially in the world's oppressed and outcast and marginalized, the face of Jesus is to be discerned. Small wonder that those whose lives are consumed by the love of Jesus should so consistently spend themselves in service to these little ones of the earth, for the truly faithful are convinced that in serving the little ones they are serving Christ, and that in learning those little ones they are in the most direct way possible learning Jesus.

CHAPTER 4

The Process of Learning Jesus

We are pursuing the implications of a strong belief in the resurrection for knowledge of Jesus. If we are dealing not with a dead person of the past but with a person whose life continues, however mysteriously, in the present, then it is better to speak of "learning Jesus" than of "knowing Jesus." We are concerned with a *process* rather than a *product*. Having sketched the framework of tradition within which such learning takes place, and having suggested some of the ways in which the resurrected Lord as life-giving Spirit continues to find embodiment in the world, we can now direct our attention to the complex process of learning Jesus within the life of faith.

Learning People

A good place to begin is with the recognition that all learning between people involves a process so complex and opaque as almost to defy analysis. For humans to learn about *things* is fairly straightforward, even though we cannot yet claim to understand such cognition in its entirety. Insofar as the things themselves stand still, however, and insofar as we can devise fair and accurate tests, we can determine—in the case of numbers and forms and ancient languages and all sorts of historical data—that people take things into themselves, as it were, and eject them again pretty much intact, not noticeably affected by having passed through a human brain. Things that live and move and grow, however, are much trickier, and learning them requires quicker feet. The more life and movement involved, in fact, the more complex the process of learning. The more complex the form of life and movement, the more difficult and slow the learning, and the more tentative and open-ended the hypotheses. The more such complexity of life involves interiority and some form of consciousness, the more the gap between how we are learning and what we are learning gets closed, the more critical become the changing positions of observer and observed, and the more flexible and responsive must be the learner. And when it is a matter of learning from and about another human person, then the process is difficult and delicate indeed.

It is important to emphasize here that I am not referring to the knowledge of humans claimed by certain proponents of the so-called social sciences, who proceed on the basis of dismissing considerations of freedom and interiority and treat humans collectively, as though they were only a slightly more disorganized hive of bees. I am not interested in challenging the validity of knowledge reached by such premises and procedures, but only in pointing out that such knowledge is gained by reducing people to the level of things and is therefore of limited value to those who seek to learn other human beings as people—that is, precisely as creatures possessing interiority and freedom. Although the social sciences tend to treat people as problems to be solved, people are in fact best learned when they are viewed as mysteries to be experienced.

This distinction between "problem" and "mystery," which I touched on briefly in Chapter 1, came to my attention through the writings of the French Catholic existentialist philosopher Gabriel Marcel. He distinguishes between the kind of thinking that is appropriate when people respond to a problem and that which is appropriate to a mystery. A problem is something that lies outside us and has a certain objective character; with enough energy, time, and intelligence, we can solve a problem. In that solution-seeking process, furthermore, it is important not to get personally involved. Budgets are best dealt with by folks who treat them as financial problems rather than as a measure of their personal worth, for example; and broken carburetors are best fixed by mechanics who have no strong opinions about the place of the internal combustion engine in the cosmos. In contrast, mysteries enter into those dimensions of human existence in which we are by definition very much involved: situations of health and sickness, birth and death, alienation and reconciliation. Because our selves are already deeply involved, we cannot detach ourselves from such situations without distorting them. If we treat grief as a problem to be solved rather than as a mystery to be experienced, then we will relate to grief in unhelpful and possibly destructive ways. In the realm of mystery, it is not the calculating intelligence of problem solving that is called for, but the meditative intelligence of reflection.

The difference between learning things and learning people has to do precisely with interiority and freedom. In the realm of learning people there is no clear demarcation between subject and object, between learner and learned. The best term to describe the capacities associated with being a subject/object in that realm is *spirit*. The spirit within humans—the human spirit—is embodied, but it is also the dimension of the human being that is capable of transcending mere bodiliness. The reality of spirit is deduced from the human activities of knowing and loving, in which that which lies outside the person is also made to be inside the person. In the case of learning people, both the learner and the one being learned are subjects: the spirit that enables one person to overleap the boundary of the body in knowledge and love and to incorporate the other in the self is matched by the same spirit in the other. The one to be learned is also alive, moving, conscious, alert, and free. The one to be learned is also (and at the same time) learning the learner, and is changing spiritually through the very process of exchange that is the learning of people between people.

The learning of another person requires certain moral as well as intellectual capacities. The first of these, in order both of occurrence and of importance, may well be *trust*. Trust is a fundamental openness to the reality of the other. It involves a certain basic acceptance of the other—a belief that the other *is*, that the other is *real*, that the other is *true*—prior to any empirical calculation. Perhaps the evidence will challenge or even subvert the premise established by trust. But without such basic openness, no learning can take place. In the absence of trust that the other will reveal herself, the learner must take up the stance of the scientist who learns only from surface appearances. It is clear also that having such trust in the other means at some level that the learner is *entrusting* herself to the other, by relinquishing the sort of control that subjects normally have over the objects they are studying.

The attitude of trust involves an element of *respect* as well. The other is not simply a thing to be grasped, measured, and catalogued. Respect means the acknowledgment of the other as truly other than the self, as equally worthy as the self, as having as much interiority and freedom as the self. Trust and respect are the fundamental premises for any personal learning. Without them, intersubjectivity is lost; the other person—the one learned—is reduced to object only. As a result, both the spirit of the learner and the spirit of the one learned are occluded.

Attentiveness is another component of intersubjective learning. It is not quite the same thing as concentration, which suggests an intense focusing of the mind in order to see or hear something "accurately." Attentiveness suggests alertness, yes, but also receptivity. It is a "leaning toward" the other. Attentiveness is present when we truly listen to the other person, when we contemplate the other person. It does not assume that the other is already known, has been "figured out." Instead, it assumes that the other is always capable of change and surprise. The attitude of attentiveness contains within itself space for the other to remain other; it does not rush to change the other or to control the other. Like trust and respect, attentiveness is a mental and moral attitude that acknowledges and accepts the freedom of the other.

To truly learn another person, it is necessary also to *meditate* on the other in *silence*. Though this reflexive move is natural and obvious when we fall in love with another person, we often forget how critical it is to all interpersonal learning. Time and space and silence are required to ponder what the other person has said or done in our presence. In such silence we can imaginatively summon the other's presence, can picture him in characteristic motion, can assess what we have just heard or seen in the light of what the other has already revealed of himself. Without such opportunities to reflect and ponder, knowledge of the other person remains episodic, disconnected, and superficial. It is in the soil of silent reflection that learning of the other puts down deep roots.

Personal learning cannot take place all at once, but only with the *passage of time*. At first acquaintance with another person, we are often tempted to "analyze" the other in an attempt to "figure her out." Generally, though, as the attitudes of trust, respect, and attentiveness continue over a period of time, we come to realize that our initial conclusions are in need of revision. Since the person keeps changing, our learning of him or her must keep pace. This means that *patience* is a necessary component in personal learning.

Hand in hand with patience comes suffering; indeed, the very word *patience* connotes suffering. The ancient Greeks saw it as axiomatic that to learn was to suffer, and they reduced that conviction to a maxim: *mathein pathein*. Why that connection? *Learning* demands *suffering* because it is painful to open the mind and the heart to new truth. Pain is the symptom of a system in disequilibrium. Physical pain results not only from the body's disease but also from the body's rapid growth or from the acquiring of new muscles and skills. Pain likewise results from the need to stretch mental muscles around new ways of viewing the world. When we are learning another person, there is also inevitably emotional pain, for the very act of entrusting our self to another means a decentering and displacement of our self-preoccupation. Furthermore, the other can violate our vulnerability and cause us pain. Both for good and for bad, for loss and for gain, personal learning is always accompanied by suffering, and patience is the virtue that makes such suffering positive and meaningful: we endure for the sake of an education.

Because personal learning takes place intersubjectively over a long period of time, it also demands *creative fidelity*. Each part of this concept—

another borrowed from Gabriel Marcel—is important. First, then, personal learning requires *fidelity*, which is the attitude of trust extended through time. To learn from another we must be loyal to the other, stick with the other, be willing to endure with the other through a variety of circumstances. Pulling away, refusing to remain attentive, abandoning the other altogether means cutting off the process of intersubjective learning. (Here again patience comes into play, for such loyalty is frequently put to the test through suffering.) But the other part of the concept of creative fidelity is equally important: to be truly faithful, one must be *creative*. This is because the other, as free subject, always changes. Loyalty to what a person used to be is not creative fidelity. Loyalty to one's ideal image of the other is not creative fidelity. Not even loyalty to one's own first commitment of loyalty is creative fidelity. Creative fidelity is the willingness to trust, be attentive to, and suffer with the other even as the other changes. It is a living process, because it is a process that goes on between two living, conscious, and free subjects.

A Personal Example

I hope that my readers—and my wife, Joy—will forgive me for attempting to give concreteness to these abstract remarks by describing how Joy and I have learned each other over our time together. That relationship is not only an example, however; more fundamentally, it is the source of my understanding of personal learning. What I know about this subject I have learned either from her or from thinking about what it means to continually learn her. We have "known each other" for more than twenty-six years; we have been married for more than twenty-three. That's a fairly significant database! If personal learning does require the passage of time, as I have suggested, we have had enough time to learn a bit.

When we met, I was a twenty-eight-year-old Benedictine monk and she was a thirty-eight-year-old divorcée and mother of six children. The path by which we came together, merged our lives, gave birth to still another child together, and guided all seven children as best we could within our very real limitations was never an easy one. And we are both very different today than when we first joined our lives: not only older and shorter and heavier and more tired, but different in our perceptions of life and our responses to it. We tend to think we have changed mostly for the better because of the way we have learned each other over the years.

What *trust* it took for Joy to risk herself and her children to a man who was ten years younger, who had never dated a woman, and who had never held a job, written a check, or purchased anything costing more than five dollars—a young man, furthermore, who was abandoning his vows to the monastic life and who had only a perilous future as a graduate student in the profoundly nonremunerative field of religious studies. What *trust* it took for me to risk myself to Joy and her family, for those same reasons— plus the fact that she was older, had grown accustomed to wealth and comfort, and was herself someone who had left a commitment of more than twenty years. The trust was not made easier by the "advice" given each of us by "friends" eager for us to stay where we were. He is unstable and flighty, immature and unreliable, Joy was told; you are only the symptom; he needs to grow up before he is ready for this sort of adult life. She is a neurotic person, I was told, whose religious piety is a defense against an inability to deal realistically with the world; look at the troubled state of her family and know that she will do the same thing again.

Yet somehow we trusted each other more than we trusted the voices of others, and we joined our lives. But what was it, really, that we were trusting? Certainly Joy did not know much "objectively" about me in the beginning, and what she did know would pretty much have confirmed what was being whispered in her ear by my detractors. Likewise, what I knew of her "objectively" was not extensive but could have been read to yield the same sort of reductive dismissal: dissatisfied and restless woman. Joy trusted what she heard in my voice. I trusted what I saw in her clear eyes. We decided together, not with words but with a simple implicit resolution, never to trust what anyone else told us about the other, but only what we learned from each other about each other. We trusted that what we saw and heard in each other was real and was truthful. And on that basis we moved forward.

I think that what we were trusting was the reality I have called *spirit*, and this in two ways. First, although we were from the beginning very much "embodied" toward each other, and remain so still, we did not relate to each other on the basis of external observation and deduction so much as on the basis of mutual self-revelation; we acknowledged each other's interiority and freedom and realized that the truth of our relationship must be based on the truth of this spiritual reality. Second, we shared the conviction that our human spirit was created and sustained and called by the *Spirit of God*, so that the prior trust each of us had placed in the truthfulness of God's Spirit in our lives found confirmation in our deep agreement on this most essential point. Whatever we were going to be together was to be with reference to our shared spiritual life, defined in terms of God's Holy Spirit.

This basic trust has been the foundation for all that we have subsequently learned from each other. As with all married couples, we were many times over the years faced with situations that invited one or the other to cancel that premise of trust, to grow suspicious, to revert to a more controlled and comfortable way of knowing from a distance, to render the other an object through observation and analysis rather than continuing to regard the other as an equal subject to be engaged in the slow and difficult process of speaking and hearing about difficult things. We came through those times on the basis of trust; and because we did, our trust thus confirmed has grown. I know with the deep moral certainty of the heart that Joy is good and true and acts for my good in every situation, and I know that she knows the same thing about me. Thus the premise of our learning each other has also been over the years the substance of what we have learned from each other.

The qualities of *respect* and *attentiveness* followed from that basic trust. Each of us, we have discovered over our years together, tends toward willfulness: we are quick to make up our minds and seek to shape the world according to our desires. It has been difficult to respect and pay attention to the other: to acknowledge the other as free subject and not simply as part of my own project. It has taken much discipline (and the learning that comes from many failures) to truly listen to each other and not close off true hearing by assuming that we already know what the other is saying. Equally difficult has been learning how to speak truly and simply, without using speech as an instrument of manipulation. For us, the commitment never to close the door on a hurt or on a failure to communicate has been fundamental. It has led to many long nights of painful struggle to speak and to be heard, but with that struggle has also come confirmation that respect and attentiveness are rewarded with the revelation of the other as other and not as a projection of either one's fantasy.

Holding each other in our hearts in *silence* and *meditation* has enabled us to learn each other at a depth that would not have otherwise been possible. For a variety of reasons, we have had to spend much time apart over the years, attending to other people's needs, going through separate pleasures and pains. But when I am on a trip lecturing or when I spend a long day in meetings, I know that I am also sustained as a presence in Joy's thoughts and prayers. She is with me as I move through airport and classroom just as I am with her as she moves through her daily round. And when Joy is away with our children or caring for her mother, she knows that the same is true: she is with me and I am with her even when we are apart. We have learned the power of this silent meditative presence in those moments when sickness or tragedy has drawn one of us into places the other could not go except through such imaginative participation, such silent presence-in-absence. I have learned Joy differently and more deeply because I have gone with her in my mind and heart through the dark valleys her body needed to walk alone. And she has learned me more profoundly because in her silent thoughts she has stood vigil with me in moments and places of crisis.

Life together always involves *suffering* and demands *patience*. Such is the case even when—at least to all appearances—life unfolds normally and predictably, for the process of intersubjective learning always involves tension, challenge, the demand to grow beyond a private space in order to inhabit a larger reality. Simply because two people are constantly themselves in the process of change and growth, their effort to grow together and to learn from each other is an exercise filled with tension and stress. The individual project of one person is inevitably intersected by the project of the other. Add more people to the mix and the potential for stress and therefore for suffering is still greater. Joy and I are ten years apart in age, came from different regions of the country, had different "first and failed commitments," and came together with substantially different experiences of education, culture, possessions, and politics. Our merged family has seven children spanning twenty years (and several generations of adolescent crises). Our decision to be together meant the disruption of Joy's first family, the abandonment of my monastic family, and—for both of us—an alienation from the religious community that had sustained us all our lives. To survive and support this life demanded more time at work (official and moonlighting) than is usually associated with a balanced lifestyle. Added to all this, we have had the peculiarly interesting challenge of chronic periodic illness during all our years together. The simplest way to say this is that we have spent far more time in hospital emergency rooms and in surgery and in long days of domestic pain than we have on vacation. While Joy and I would concur with the Greek maxim that to learn is to suffer, we would add also that to suffer is to learn. We have found that suffering together educates us in a knowledge of each other and an appreciation for each other in a way that a life less filled with challenge would not have. We have learned in our bones that suffering with and for the other is a way God opens up a space for God's own freedom in our hearts.

Finally, Joy and I have found out how necessary *creative fidelity* is to our learning from and with each other as people. Each of us changes, if only slightly, every day. And over the many years together, each of us has changed quite a lot. Our loyalty to each other has had to be expressed in the willingness to change with and for the other. This need to be creative in order to be truly loyal has enabled each of us also to discover capacities within ourselves that we had not thought were there. The willingness to let the other be creative—that is, to change and grow, sometimes in quite unexpected ways—has invited each of us also to be creative and to grow.

Let me offer a few final comments on the loving and learning relationship between Joy and me before returning to the main topic of learning Jesus. The first comment is that the farther one goes into the learning process, the clearer it becomes not only how complex the process has been, but also how impossible it is to put the resulting learning into a neat formula. When we first met, I could have provided a fairly good description of Joy, and I am sure she could have of me as well. But now, although I know her dear face better than my own, I would not be able to be so definite: her face in which of the thousand moments and moods we have been together? Likewise with her behavior: an anecdote demonstrating one characteristic makes me think at once of another demonstrating the opposite characteristic. What a complex person this simple person is! And how impossible it is to render personal learning of this sort in the categories of ordinary cognition. I am always startled by the fact that the Joy in photographs looks so little like *my* Joy. She does not photograph well, it is true, but my reaction is also connected to the fact that I never experience her as frozen in time and space: she is a living presence, and I never see her "objectively"—nor do I desire that.

Second, I hope that the reader understands that neither Joy nor I can pretend to have this personal learning process mastered. It looks much better in hindsight than it does in day-to-day life together. We are not models of much of anything—certainly not of the ideal marriage or relationship. Our frailties and failings are as glaringly obvious to us as they are to our children and friends. But I do think we exemplify some of the complexity of the process of personal learning, and we have committed ourselves to the attitudes and qualities that make such learning possible, even though we are very much a work in progress.

Finally, I have given this much attention to the process of personal learning between Joy and me because, for me, it is not simply *analogous* to how we learn Jesus; it has been for the past twenty-five years the most important context in which I have continued to learn Jesus. I would embarrass Joy needlessly to spell this out, so I will simply state that what I have called the pattern of Jesus' identity—namely, a life of self-giving service in which the process of dying gives life—is one that I have learned above all from my partner in faith and love.

Learning Jesus

The process of learning Jesus must be, for each individual person who undertakes it, even more complex than the process of learning another human being. The elements of all intersubjective learning are present, yet in distinctive ways that make learning between two humans analogous rather than identical.

The reality of the *spirit* that enables all intersubjective learning in this case involves on one side the human spirit, with its capacities for knowing and loving, and on the other side the Holy Spirit of God, which mediates the presence of the risen Jesus to humans. It is the spirit of humans, says Paul, that enables them "to know a person's thoughts"; it is God's Spirit that "searches everything, even the depths of God" (1 Cor. 2:10–11). Because humans are gifted with that divine Spirit, they are able to "comprehend the thoughts of God" and thereby to "understand the gifts bestowed on [them] by God" (1 Cor. 2:11–12). The mutuality of knowing and being known is thus much deeper (1 Cor. 8:1–3), even if it cannot be articulated, for the Spirit of God is more interior to us, as Augustine declares, than we are to ourselves. Because by his resurrection Jesus has become life-giving Spirit, he is able to know and to be known in a manner impossible to him when confined to his mortal body.

Such spiritual intimacy is intimated but not adequately expressed by those passages in the New Testament that speak of Christians being "in Christ" (1 Thess. 4:16; 1 Cor. 15:22; 2 Cor. 5:17; Phil. 2:1; Col. 1:2) or of Christ being "in them" (Col. 1:27; Eph. 3:17). Paul's language concerning his own relationship to the risen Lord is most emphatic: "It is no longer I who live, but Christ who lives in me" (Gal. 2:20). That language is not far from the wording used by John for the mutual indwelling of Jesus and his friends: "Remain in me and I in you. As the branch cannot bear fruit by itself unless it abides in the vine, neither can you unless you remain in me" (John 15:4). In his last prayer for the disciples, Jesus petitions (through John's pen) "that they may all be one, even as you Father are in me and I in you, that they may also be in us, so that the world may believe that you have sent me. . . . I in them and you in me, that they may become perfectly one" (John 17:20–23). To affirm the reality of Jesus' resurrection life is to affirm also that in the Spirit Jesus can both know and be known.

The element of *trust* is even more critical here than it is in the case of other interpersonal learning. We need to have trust first of all that Jesus is raised from the dead, lives now as powerful Lord, and is available to us in the Spirit, even though appearances and the laws of probability do not support that conviction. We need to trust, furthermore, that the means by which Jesus has chosen to communicate with us are reliable: that the portrayal of him in the Gospels is not the result of the early church's malicious manipulation or fundamental misunderstanding, for example, or that the entire tradition of creed and teaching is not so corrupt that it distorts Jesus entirely, or that the encounter with Jesus through Meal and Word and

Saint and Stranger is not mere fantasy or projection. In short, our trust is directed not only to Jesus but also to the ways in which Jesus has entrusted himself to humans. We place our trust in the process of communication through the power of the Spirit and the ways in which the Spirit finds embodiment.

As in other interpersonal learning, such trust can be severely tested. When the power of the Spirit is not obviously present, it is tempting to place trust elsewhere. When the witnesses that embody the Spirit's presence are damaged or distorting, it is difficult to sustain loyalty. We can grow discouraged, disenchanted, even at times disengaged. At such times, we are tempted to seek some other means of securing knowledge about Jesus than those means through which he has chosen to reveal himself; we yearn to find some leverage over tradition by uncovering some "objective" knowledge of Jesus not dependent on the fragile trustworthiness of the witnesses chosen by Jesus to embody his presence in the world. Giving in to such temptation, however, means stepping outside the realm of interpersonal learning. It makes Jesus an object rather than another subject. It seeks to know him as we know a thing rather than as we know other people.

Our trust is directed toward God as well—trust that in Jesus has been truly disclosed the truth about human life and the truth about God, so that if we entrust ourselves to God through Jesus we shall not be led astray or utterly lose ourselves. We trust that in Jesus God has truly shown us the "way and the truth and the life" (John 14:6), that in Jesus we truly perceive the "pioneer and perfecter of faith" (Heb. 12:3), that in Jesus "made perfect" we see "the source of eternal salvation to all who obey him" (Heb. 5:9). We trust that "God was in Christ reconciling the world to himself" (5:19) and believe that by placing our trust in Jesus (and the way toward God that Jesus has revealed through his own faithful obedience), we shall have "entrusted our lives to a faithful creator" (1 Pet. 4:19).

Trust is a dimension of that attitude usually called *faith*. The author of Hebrews says of faith that it is "the substance of things hoped for, the conviction of things not seen" (11:1), and declares concerning God that "without faith it is impossible to please him. For whoever would draw near to God must believe that God exists and that God rewards those who seek him" (11:6). Our "faith in Christ Jesus" (Col. 1:5) is our way of articulating faith in God, out of the conviction that God has revealed, in Christ, the perfect pattern of faith and that "He who raised Christ Jesus from the dead will give life to [our] mortal bodies also through his Spirit that dwells in [us]" (Rom. 8:11).

I stated earlier the need for *respect* in all interpersonal learning. In the case of learning Jesus, this respect is not simply the recognition of the other as a spiritual and free being; it involves the recognition that in Jesus we have to do with the Holy One of God. Our faith in Jesus therefore is more than simple trust; it is also made up of the fear of the Lord and of *obedience*. When we attempt to learn Jesus, we are not in an egalitarian relationship; on the contrary, the most profound humility and submission on our part are appropriate. Jesus is not for us simply an interesting figure of the past about whom any opinion is valid, any attitude is acceptable; rather, Jesus is the one whom "God has highly exalted and [on whom God has] bestowed the name which is above every name, that at the name of Jesus every knee should bow, in heaven and on earth and under the earth, and every tongue confess that Jesus Christ is Lord to the glory of God the Father" (Phil. 2:9–11, RSV). Therefore, the appropriate attitude for learning Jesus is to "reverence Christ as Lord in your hearts" (1 Pet. 3:15).

The posture of *attentiveness* is likewise more imperative in learning Jesus than in other intersubjective learning. Other people, after all, are finite in their spiritual energy, and despite their capacity to surprise, they tend to fall into routines and predictable patterns. In relationships with people, then, occasional downtime is possible. But the resurrected Jesus—

the embodiment of life-giving Spirit—possesses the energy of God's own life. The Letter to the Hebrews gives particular attention to the need for attentiveness to the word of God spoken by Christ: "Today if you hear his voice, do not harden your hearts as in the rebellion" (Heb. 3:7; citing Ps. 95:8). God continues to speak through Jesus with a word that calls humans into judgment:

> For the word of God is living and active, sharper than any two-edged sword, piercing to the division of soul and spirit, of joints and marrow, and discerning the thoughts and intentions of the heart. And before him no creature is hidden, but all are open and laid bare to the eyes of him with whom we have to do. (Heb. 4:12–13, RSV)

The response of faith in Jesus demands the asceticism of attentiveness, for "it is a fearful thing to fall into the hands of the living God" (Heb. 10:31). The relationship with Jesus is neither comfortable nor altogether comforting. It challenges us and even frightens us with its demand that we be transformed according to the image of the one who has gone before us and continues to press upon us. Hebrews says again:

> You have come . . . to Jesus, the mediator of a new covenant, and to the sprinkled blood that speaks more graciously than the blood of Abel. See that you do not refuse him who is speaking. For if they did not escape when they refused him who warned them on earth, much less shall we escape if we reject him who warns from heaven. . . . [T]hus let us offer to God acceptable worship with reverence and awe, for our God is a consuming fire. (Heb. 12:22–29, RSV)

Because the risen Lord is not an embodied subject in the same manner that other people are, the role of *silence* and *meditation* in learning Jesus is of critical importance. Neither Jesus' absence nor his presence can be measured like that of other people. His presence is often mediated and indirect and the learning from that presence is therefore oblique. His apparent absence is particularly hard to assess, for as many mystics have shown, the movement into an ever deeper relationship with Jesus leads from a comforting sense of a palpable presence through the dark night of the senses and the dark night of the soul, in which the subject of our human longing and love seems to recede even as we approach. Without silence and meditation, the learning of Jesus lacks the depth of personal appropriation. Silent prayer serves to purify the process of our learning, winnowing away the chaff of opinion and speculation and noisy chatter and verbal polemics to reveal bit by bit the pure grain of authentic knowing.

Learning Jesus inevitably involves suffering and therefore requires *patience*. The learning of Jesus is not simply the acquiring of facts or even of insight; rather, it is a matter of being conformed to the image of the one known. Paul hopes to "know him and the power of his resurrection, and share his sufferings, becoming like him in his death, that I might somehow attain the resurrection from the dead" (Phil. 3:11). All learning, I have suggested, demands some suffering. All interpersonal learning in particular involves the suffering that results from the clash between two or more freedoms at work. In the case of learning Jesus, however, there is not only that suffering intrinsic to learning itself—the stretching of the self in order to reach a higher place—but also the suffering that results as a life is shaped by the Spirit of Jesus into conformity with the pattern of obedience and self-giving love that he himself displayed.

It is the dimension of suffering, not as something chosen out of masochism but as an element of growth in the Spirit itself, that distinguishes authentic learning of Jesus from cheap versions of Christianity that trumpet Jesus as the solution to all life's problems. The mark of genuine discipleship is the suffering that begins when the learning of Jesus is truly undertaken. Paul expresses the confidence that Jesus "will change our lowly body to be like his glorious body, by the power that empowers him also to subject all things to himself" (Phil. 3:21), but that transformation is one that must pass, as did Jesus himself, through suffering to glory (Luke 24:26; 1 Pet. 1:11).

Part of the suffering of discipleship derives from the fact that our trust and obedience are directed toward a being who, as the Living One, always moves ahead of us. Our learning, then, must be continuous. We cannot ever stop and say that we "know Jesus"; we can only move forward in the process of "learning Jesus." We are not allowed the luxury of certainty, but only the pain of ambiguity that is the lot of all learners as they move from one point of secure knowledge to another. We suffer because we are always in transition, always in a condition of stress, always free at every moment to stop or turn back or close our ears. In learning Jesus, therefore, we must above all have *creative fidelity* if our faith is to be authentic. We cannot rest content with the understanding of Jesus that was ours as children, or even the understanding of Jesus that was ours yesterday. The living Lord continues to call us beyond our present place of comfort into a life that is both infinitely richer and unspeakably more frightening.

Finally, our learning of Jesus cannot take place all at once, but can only grow over the course of time. Unlike the study of a historical figure, which comes to a resolution once all the evidence has been amassed and analyzed, our learning of Jesus continues over time as we engage the Spirit of the risen Lord at every moment of our lives. And unlike those Christians who claim to receive an immediate and adequate grasp of Jesus in a single instant of conversion—a knowledge that need never be revisited or revised and that provides a blueprint for all subsequent actions—we must claim a more modest process that goes on through every moment of life. Our fidelity is not to our past understanding but to the living Lord, which means that our learning Jesus continues as long as we live.

Learning Together

Because I have spoken throughout this chapter of learning Jesus as though it were an individual matter, I need to emphasize in conclusion the importance of the context of tradition. Learning Jesus is always a personal process, to be sure, but it is not simply an individual process. The learning must be personal to be real, but if it is only individual, then it runs the risk of being idiosyncratic and perhaps even distorted. The potential for self-deception and delusion in the spiritual life is obvious and notorious. Any talk about learning Jesus must therefore be placed firmly within the context of the community of the church, where the learning of each individual can interact with the learning of others, and where the movement of the Holy Spirit in such learning can be subject to discernment.

The First Letter of John warns against self-deception, particularly in the learning of Jesus:

> Beloved, do not believe every spirit, but test the spirits to see if they are of God; for many false prophets have gone out into the world. By this you know the Spirit of God: every spirit that confesses that Jesus Christ has come in the flesh is of God, and every spirit that does not confess Jesus is not of God. (1 John 4:1–3, RSV)

John here draws on the community's shared understanding of Jesus as the measure by which to test individual expressions of faith. Such discernment is a necessary component of life in the Spirit. It can also be abused, as when a rigid attachment to verbal orthodoxy replaces an openness to the work of the Spirit in teaching Jesus to the church. But without discernment, every sort of bizarre fantasy can pass itself off as divine revelation. The power and the presence of the risen Lord, however, are not for the satisfaction of private projections. They are for the transformation of the world.

CHAPTER 5

The Living Jesus and the Revelatory Text

Given that this book's subtitle is "Learning the Heart of the Gospel," perhaps readers are wondering when we will begin to reflect on the Jesus portrayed in the Gospels. The word *euangelion* (the Greek word that we translate as "gospel"), however, encompasses more than the literary narratives about Jesus that we call Gospels. The original meaning of *euangelion*—and the meaning still conveyed by *gospel* in its lowercase form —was the "good news from and about God," meaning above all the good news of what God has done through the death and resurrection of Jesus (see Acts 15:7; Rom. 1:1; 15:16; 1 Thess. 2:2, 8; 1 Pet. 4:17). It is in this sense that our thinking about spirituality is "gospel-centered": Christian spirituality begins with God's Holy Spirit given through the resurrection of Jesus. To be gospel-centered, therefore, means not simply to focus on the Gospel narratives and the image of Jesus found in them, but to engage the Holy Spirit in all of life's complexity. We are starting in the right place, then, if we begin by considering our relationship with Jesus as mediated by the Holy Spirit.

In addressing our learning of Jesus in the context of the church, we have also already drawn upon the Gospel texts and shown in multiple ways how they are to be engaged. This point in particular deserves emphasis: our learning of Jesus does not take place apart from the texts of Scripture that speak of him, nor is it simply derived directly from those texts. The learning of Jesus takes place by means of an extended and intense conversation involving (1) our experiences of the risen Lord—experiences that are shaped by those texts and in turn shape our reading of them—and (2) the reading of texts speaking about Jesus—texts that are shaped by our experience of him in the world and in turn shape our perception of those experiences.

That conversation is neither new nor distinctive to this generation. In fact, it began with the resurrection experience itself. The powerful presence of the transforming Spirit among Jesus' followers helped to elicit, select, and shape their memories of him, just as those memories in turn gave shape to their corporate identity and practices in the church. The writings of the New Testament themselves resulted from this process within communities. They represent for all subsequent readers a crystallization of reflection on the person of Jesus in light of the experience of the resurrection. The New Testament does not confront us as something alien, therefore, but offers an invitation to embrace and enter into the same conversation it initiated concerning the identity of that Jesus whom we experience as life-giving Spirit.

Revelatory Texts

Such an appreciation affects the way scriptural texts are approached and appropriated within the contemporary conversation. Christians for whom Jesus is living Lord turn to the texts seeking a revelation of the person of Jesus. They regard the compositions of the New Testament together and separately not as inadequate sources for historical recovery—as the historical Jesus questers do—but as invaluable witnesses to a living reality. They do not criticize the compositions or dismiss them as obstacles to the knowledge of Jesus—again, as the historical Jesus questers do—but rather honor them as indispensable enablers of the process of learning Jesus. For most Christians, then, approaching Jesus is not a matter of bypassing these compositions or correcting them in order to reach an elusive figure of the past whom the New Testament writers have fundamentally distorted. Because Jesus is present to Christians right now—as living Lord—they see the New Testament not as the record of a historical figure from the distant past but as an enriching revelation of the nature of the Messiah.

Given that perspective, those seeking to learn Jesus as the living Lord approach the New Testament not with suspicion but with trust. They believe that its compositions can truthfully reveal something of the mystery that is Jesus. Such readers embrace the testimony to Jesus given by the entire canon, recognizing that the shape of the testimony will differ according to the perspective and literary form of each composition within the canon. Approaching the text within the framework of the church's tradition and creed, such readers are prepared to find some of their perceptions about Jesus confirmed but are willing also to have some of their accustomed understandings challenged and even altered.

An attitude of openness, trust, and receptivity does not mean that readers of the New Testament must abandon all critical faculties, only that critical intelligence must be exercised within the framework of loyalty and respect. Take, for example, the most basic issue that every reader must inevitably confront—namely, the diversity of testimony concerning Jesus. The compositions simply do not speak with one voice, even about this most central figure. Readers are thus faced with a basic choice. Will they refuse to acknowledge this diversity and insist on collapsing all the voices into one? Will they instead claim that the diversity is so profound as to resist any harmonization, so that it is necessary to choose one or several witnesses as more adequate while rejecting all the others? Will they, like contemporary questers after the historical Jesus, reject all the compositions as unreliable, seeking instead to salvage some trustworthy fragments from the deconstructed compositions that might point truly to Jesus "as he was"? Or will they recognize that each of the compositions—human interpretations of a person whose life, death, and resurrection far exceeded the normal categories of human experience—has genuine value as testimony to some particular facet of Jesus, but none of them alone (nor all of them together) adequately or comprehensively captures the living reality that is Jesus?

I choose the last option. I approach these writings as thoroughly human in their composition—and therefore necessarily limited in the ways all human writings are limited—but also as inspired by the Holy Spirit of Jesus himself—and therefore able to speak truly within their limited perspective and comprehension. I assume that none of these writings tells us everything that we would like to know—some of them, indeed, tell us little or nothing about Jesus—but that each of them individually speaks truly as it is able and all of them taken together speak reliably concerning the person in whose name they were written. I make no apology for this decision, and I gladly recognize that it is a decision based upon a prior conviction of faith. But if I did not start from such a faith, it is difficult to understand why I would be seeking to learn Jesus in this personal fashion anyway.

As we turn to the writings of the New Testament, then, we do so in search of an answer not to *every* question but only to the question of how we can learn Jesus. Before turning to the four canonical Gospels, I will begin with those writings of the canon in which the story of Jesus is not the explicit topic. These writings are concerned primarily with the ways in which an identity shaped by a commitment to Jesus can consistently be lived in the world. Their explicit focus is the story of Jesus as continued in the lives of the believers. Nevertheless, many different dimensions of Jesus himself are revealed in these compositions. What they tell us is of particular value precisely because in them the image of Jesus is *assumed* more than consciously *constructed*.

These writings take the form of letters. Even the Book of Revelation, which is properly categorized as an apocalyptic writing, contains seven letters addressed to seven churches in Asia Minor and has epistolary elements framing the entire composition (see 1:4; 22:21). The majority of the compositions cannot be securely located in either time or place. We usually assume that Paul's letters are our earliest extant Christian writings, but compositions such as Hebrews, 1 Peter, James and even Jude may well have been written as early as Paul's. Certainly 2 Peter is a later document, but the letters of John are impossible to date. It is safe to assert that all of them were composed from within and for Christian communities in the last five decades of the first century, however, and that many of them antedate the Gospels.

The reader should be warned that the usual preoccupations of historical criticism are here being bracketed. Although for some purposes it makes a great deal of difference indeed whether a letter was written in this circumstance or in that, for our present purposes it makes virtually no difference. We are not trying to evaluate the overall composition, after all; we are concerned only with its portrayal of Jesus. Regardless of the circumstances leading to that portrayal, our interest is only in the result. We will assess, then, the particular emphases of the respective texts as well as the ways they converge. Even as we seek the image of Jesus in each writing or collection of writings, however, we must acknowledge the limits of the enterprise. Neither alone nor together are these texts adequate to the reality of Jesus; our assessment of them is therefore less definitive than suggestive.

For each composition I will indicate the distinctive designations of Jesus, the ways in which his present reality and his relationship to believers is stated, the future role he is assigned, the discussion of his past deeds and their significance, and the relationship drawn between discipleship and the humanity of Jesus.

REVELATION

I begin with Revelation, the scriptural writing that probably seems strangest even to its most obsessive perusers, for the literary conventions of ancient apocalypticism are no longer widely appreciated. One of these conventions involves casting human characters as animals, a technique not unlike that of contemporary cartoons. Thus Revelation's most distinctive representation of Jesus is as a lamb (5:6, 12; 7:14, 16–17; 12:11; 13:9; 14:1; 17:14; 19:7–9; 21:10; 22:1–3)—a symbolism that not only fits within the characterization of other figures as beasts, but also specifically echoes the rich biblical tradition of the paschal lamb and the prophetic comparison of God's suffering servant to the lamb who is led to the slaughter. Note, for example, the hymn sung in heaven by the four living creatures and the twenty-four elders before the lamb: "Worthy art thou to take the scroll and open its seals, for thou wast slain and by thy blood didst ransom people for God from every tribe and tongue and people and nation, and hast made them a kingdom of priests to our God, and they shall reign on earth" (Rev. 5:9–10, RSV). In fact, however—although the lamb is clearly meant to represent Jesus—that link is neither explicitly made by the text nor typically challenged by readers. It is because this lamb's death was in ransom for others that the reader automatically identifies the lamb with Jesus. The clustering of associations around a certain symbol compels identification with a specific figure.

Jesus does receive a full range of other titles as well: he is "Son of man" (1:3) and "Son of God" (1:9); he is "Messiah" (11:15) and "Lord" (22:20)—indeed, he is "Lord of lords and King of kings" (17:14). Jesus is the "Word of God" (19:17), testifying (1:2) as the faithful and true witness (3:14). In a string of epithets that cover the range of his past and present activity, Jesus is called "faithful witness, first born of the dead, ruler of all the kings of earth" (1:5).

As the "first born of the dead" (1:5), the one who was "slain but now lives" (1:18), Jesus is supremely the Living One and Lord. He is present in the midst of the churches (1:19; 2:1), knows what is happening in them (2:2), and through the Spirit of prophecy speaks to them (2:7, 11, 29): "And write to the Angel of the church in Philadelphia: 'Thus says the Holy One, the True One, who has the key of David, who opens and no one shall shut, who shuts and no one opens'" (3:7). He is the judge who will reward and punish those in the churches (2:7, 17, 26; 3:21). As the Living One, Jesus testifies to the churches (1:2) and reveals to them what will shortly happen (1:1). Jesus continues to have an active role in the world beyond the churches: he will do battle with the evil powers in the world (19:11, 17–21) and will exercise dominion with the saints (20:4–6).

The significance of Jesus' humanity is equally real: he was born of a woman as a male child (12:5). As noted, he is the "faithful witness" even before his resurrection (1:8). Indeed, Jesus witnesses as a prophet. In a statement that captures much of the point of this complex writing, the reader is told, "The spirit of prophecy is the testimony of Jesus" (19:10). The Greek genitive is typically ambiguous here in the phrase "testimony of Jesus," capable of being rendered also as "testimony *to* Jesus." (See below, page 84.) Jesus' life and death are epitomized in terms of self-donation: "He loves us and freed us from our sins by his blood" (1:5). The fact that Jesus did not die a natural death but was "slain" is emphasized (5:12). His death is portrayed in sacrificial terms derived from Torah; thus he "purchased" humans by his blood (5:9) and "purified" them (7:14). There is a clear allusion to Jesus' death in Jerusalem; speaking of the "two witnesses" whose pattern of prophecy resembles that of Jesus, Revelation refers to the city "spiritually called Sodom and Egypt *where their Lord was crucified*" (11:8, italics added). This same Jesus is the Risen One, the "first born of the dead" (1:8), who was "snatched up to God and to his throne" (12:5), the one who "was dead and now lives" (1:18).

The image of Jesus as lamb communicates the same progression: the lamb "was slaughtered from the creation of the world" (13:8), washes the saints in its blood (7:14), and will shepherd the saints (7:17). The "wrath of the lamb" (7:16–17) expresses God's commitment to judge the nations with justice and make war against the powers of wickedness (19:11). The saints await the future triumph of the lamb (19:7–9; 21:10, 21–22; 22:1–3). But they also "follow the lamb wherever he goes" (14:4–5). They too have that "spirit of prophecy" that is their "witness to Jesus" (19:10). They disseminate in the world the same testimony that Jesus bore to God: they "hold God's commandments and hold to the testimony of Jesus" (12:17). Thus they are able to conquer the rulers of this earth through "the blood of the lamb and their testimony" (12:11). Like Jesus, they refuse to accept the powers of the world as ultimate, worshiping only God (19:10; 22:9). This is their testimony and their most provocative political posture. And because the world resists such truthful testimony, they will also undergo the sufferings that Jesus did. Learning Jesus therefore means "patient endurance and faithfulness on the part of the saints" (13:10), phrasing later repeated as "patient endurance on the part of the saints who obey God's commandments and remain faithful to Jesus" (14:12). Although they await the return of Jesus in triumph and pray, "Come, Lord Jesus" (22:20), the saints live a life of witness to the truth, empowered by the spirit of prophecy that comes from the risen Jesus and that carries on the testimony borne by the human Jesus.

THE LETTER OF JUDE

The Letter of Jude is so obscure in its origins, so small in size, and so single-minded in its focus that it is a puzzle why it was included in the canon of Scripture. Included it was, though, and it remains a potent expression of outrage at a libertinism that "turns grace into a license for immorality" (2). For the author of Jude, people who divide communities by their immoral behavior demonstrably "follow mere natural instincts and do not have the Spirit" (19). In contrast, Jude exhorts his readers to "build yourselves up in your most holy faith and pray in the Holy Spirit" (20).

What is most striking in this tiny composition of a mere twenty-five verses is that Jesus is named six times. Jude first identifies himself as a "servant of Jesus Christ" (1). ("Christ" is attached to every occurrence of "Jesus" in Jude, as if it were part of his name rather than a title ascribed to him.) Given Jude's self-designation as "servant," it is not surprising to find Jesus called "Lord" four times (4. 17. 21. 25) and "sovereign" once (4). Jude refers to Jesus' human life when he alludes to the predictions made by "the apostles of our Lord Jesus Christ" (17): "They said to you, 'In the last time there will be mockers, following their own ungodly passions'" (18).

Jesus' future activity is stated in verse 21: "You wait for the mercy of our Lord Jesus Christ to bring you to eternal life." But it is his present power and presence that are especially stressed, making it clear that Jesus is "Lord" in the fullness of resurrection life. It is Jesus who "keeps" the community (1), just as God "keeps" them from falling (24). It is Jesus through whom the community offers its praise to God (25). Above all, Jesus is the grace or gift that is given to humans by God. Note that Jude's charge that some have changed the grace of God into a license for immorality is equivalent to "denying Jesus Christ our only master and Lord" (4).

To learn Jesus in Jude, then, is to recognize that he is the powerful presence of God gracing human life through the Holy Spirit. Discipleship means living a life consonant with "God's love" (21). This service of obedience is keeping "the faith that was once for all handed on to the saints" (3): "But you, beloved, build yourselves up on your most holy faith; pray in the Holy Spirit; keep yourselves in the love of God; wait for the mercy of Our Lord Jesus Christ unto eternal life" (20, RSV).

2 PETER

The closest literary relation to 2 Peter in the New Testament is not 1 Peter, which was certainly written by some other author (perhaps the apostle himself), but the Letter of Jude, which bears a strong resemblance in tone and whose theme is substantially incorporated into the second chapter of 2 Peter. Like Jude, this composition—perhaps the latest written within the canon—emphasizes Jesus' present life and power. Peter is once again the "servant of Jesus Christ" (1:1), and Jesus is consistently designated as "Lord" (1:2, 8, 11, 14, 16; 2:20; 3:18). Jesus is also called "Savior" five times

(1:1, 11; 2:20; 3:2, 18). Although the title "Savior" can be used to point back to what Jesus did in the past, the emphasis in 2 Peter is on the present. The author of 2 Peter is concerned that his readers be not "ineffective and unproductive" in their "knowledge [or recognition] of the Lord Jesus Christ" (1:8). If their faith grows into goodness, knowledge, self-control, perseverance, godliness, brotherly kindness, and love (1:5–7), then they will not be unproductive and "will receive a richly prepared entry into the eternal kingdom of our Lord and Savior Jesus Christ" (1:11).

The problem addressed by 2 Peter is posed by the connection between Jesus' promise in the past and his coming in the future. The fact that Jesus had not yet returned enabled some scoffers to question the very reality of God's involvement in the world and the reliability of the divine word (3:3–4). The letter therefore seeks to reassure its readers that the words spoken in the past by the prophets and "the command given by our Lord and Savior through your apostles" (3:2) were not empty but will come to fulfillment. The trustworthiness of Jesus' own words is certified by the experience of Peter himself. Clearly referring to the incident known as the transfiguration—an incident also reported in the Synoptic Gospels (Mark 9:2–8; Matt. 17:1–8; Luke 9:28–36)—the author states:

> We were eyewitnesses of his majesty; for when he received honor and glory from God the Father when the voice came to him from the majestic glory saying, "This is my Son whom I love, with him I am well pleased," we ourselves heard this voice when we were with him on the sacred mountain. (2 Pet. 1:16–18)

Even more than that, Peter has been told by "our Lord Jesus Christ" that Peter is to die soon, and therefore he "knows" that he will soon put aside the tent of the body (1:13–14). We see in this passage how the experience of Jesus in the past and the experience of his living presence in the present cooperate in providing a sense of hope concerning his coming in the future. The task for those who are followers of Jesus in the present, however, is to be on guard against those who would lead them astray, and to "grow in the grace and knowledge of our Lord and Savior Jesus Christ" and thus by their lives to express the praise with which 2 Peter closes: "To him be glory both now and forever, Amen!" (3:18).

THE LETTER OF JAMES

Sometime in the first generation of Christianity, a leader of the church in Jerusalem—perhaps James the brother of Jesus—wrote to those "in the twelve tribes of the Diaspora" (1:1), calling them to a single-minded dedication to the faith and love that they professed (1:8; 4:8). Readers have always been startled at the apparent lack of attention given to Jesus in this witness to primitive Christianity. Jesus' name appears only in the greeting of 1:1 and in 2:1. Some scholars have even theorized that James was a Jewish composition to which the name of Jesus was awkwardly added later. That view is surely wrong, for although James's approach to Jesus is distinctive, it is no less significant than that of other New Testament writings.

First, while the name of Jesus occurs only twice, it does so in critical connections. In both instances, Jesus is identified as "Lord." In the greeting, James calls himself a "servant [or slave] of God and of the Lord Jesus Christ." The title "Lord" corresponds to James's devotion and service as slave. It is clear, therefore, that James recognizes Jesus as the Living One in whose service he himself lives. In 2:1, furthermore, the practice of discrimination between members of the community is declared incompatible with "the faith of our glorious Lord Jesus Christ." James is proposing that "faith" as a measure of reality opposes "the world" (see 2:5), and that this faith is most intimately connected with Jesus, either as its source or as its object. Both James himself and the community of his readers are therefore called to a life measured by the one who is "glorious Lord" (or "Lord of glory")—that is, the resurrected Jesus, whose "noble name has been invoked upon them" (2:7).

In this light, James's other uses of the title "Lord" are intriguing.

87

Sometimes he manifestly refers to God (see 3:9; 4:15), but in other instances it is Jesus whom he refers to as Lord; see especially his references to the "coming [parousia] of the Lord" (5:7) and to the expectation, regarding the sick person, that "the Lord will raise him up" (5:15). James's language in such places echoes that of the Gospels.

Second, although James does not speak explicitly of the death and resurrection of Jesus, or of the gift of the Holy Spirit—here is where the letter's real distinctiveness lies—he does make rich use of sayings of Jesus known to us from the Gospels. James does not identify these sayings as coming from Jesus; he simply weaves them into his own discourse. And scholars debate exactly how many of these sayings can actually be detected. Some are obvious, such as the citation of the "royal law of love" in 2:8 (see Lev. 19:18; Matt 22:39) and the condemnation of oaths in 5:12: "But above all, my brothers, do not swear, either by heaven or by earth or with any other oath, but let your yes be yes and your no be no, that you may not fall under condemnation" (compare Matt. 5:33–37). Others are more subtle, though still certain, such as the allusion to the first beatitude in 2:5: "Listen, my beloved brothers, has not God chosen the poor in the world to be rich in faith and to be heirs of the kingdom he promised to those who love him?" (compare Luke 6:20; Matt. 5:3). Still others are debatable. But no one who has read James carefully can avoid the impression that this letter breathes the air of the Sermon on the Mount. Compare, for example, James 1:5 and Matthew 7:7.

In James, then, learning Jesus is not a matter of knowing facts about his life, or even of celebrating what God has accomplished through his death and resurrection. Learning Jesus means living out the faith of Jesus and the love of Jesus with single-minded consistency, using as guides to such practice the words of Torah and the very words of Jesus himself. Thus Jesus' command to love the neighbor as the self (2:8) is spelled out in terms of an active faith that shares possessions with the needy—showing the sort of faith demonstrated by Abraham and Rahab (2:18–26). Faith that is not put into practice—that is, "faith apart from deeds"—is "dead" (2:26) and certainly not to be identified with "the faith of our Lord Jesus Christ, of glory" (2:1).

THE LETTERS OF JOHN

It is not possible to identify precisely either the source or the audience of these compositions, which were probably written as a three-letter packet to readers in the midst of a serious crisis generated by disagreements concerning the proper understanding of Jesus. Two of them are genuine letters sent from a certain "elder": one to a local leader of a house church (3 John), the other to the community itself (2 John). The longest (1 John), more of a treatise than a letter, is probably the "something written for the church" that is mentioned in 3 John 9. The compositions have been connected to "John" since antiquity and certainly resemble the Fourth Gospel in language and perspective; they are rightly considered part of the literature deriving from and addressed to that form of Christianity that looked to the "disciple whom Jesus loved" as its apostle (see John 13:23; 19:35; 21:20).

Although 3 John does not mention Jesus at all, readers familiar with the other two letters would know that its praise for those "walking in the truth" (3 John 4) applies to those living according to the proper understanding of Jesus. In 2 John, Jesus is the Son of God: the greeting expresses assurance that "grace, mercy, peace, will be with us from God who is Father and from Jesus Christ the Son of the Father in truth and love" (2 John 3). It follows, therefore, that those who "remain in this teaching have both the Father and the Son" (2 John 9). In contrast, those "deceivers who went out into the world" from the community "do not confess that Jesus Christ has come in the flesh"; they are further identified as "the deceiver and the antichrist" (2 John 7). This is all very cryptic, but 2 John says enough to let us know that the proper "learning of Jesus" must recognize both the way in which he is to God as a Son is to a Father (serving therefore as the source of those spiritual benefits that God alone can bestow), and the way in which

89

he is truly human ("having come in the flesh"—which in John's lexicon means humanity in its fullness and frailty).

In 1 John these themes are woven throughout. Thus in the opening, the fellowship shared by the author and readers is one "with the Father and with his Son Jesus Christ" (1 John 1:3); and the letter concludes, "We know that the Son of God has come and has given us an understanding so that we can know the truth; and we are in the truth in his Son Jesus Christ. He is the true God and life eternal" (5:20). The letter is concerned that Jesus be recognized in all the fullness of his being and work: he is Son of God (4:15; 5:5) and Christ (5:1). The "liar," in contrast, denies that Jesus is the Christ (2:22). As one who shares the life of God, Jesus in the present stands as the advocate before God on behalf of humans (2:1). Indeed, "God has given us eternal life and this life is in his Son. The one who has the Son has life; the one who does not have the Son of God does not have life" (5:11–12).

It is the humanity of Jesus that appears to be disputed within this community, however, and therefore it is the full humanity and human work of Jesus that 1 John stresses. The presence of a Spirit from God can be discerned by its acknowledgment that "Jesus Christ has come in the flesh," whereas the sign of a spirit not from God is "not to acknowledge Jesus" (4:2–3). Jesus Christ came through water and through blood (5:6). It was the blood of Jesus that purified the believers of all sin (1:7). His death was an atoning sacrifice for their sins and the sins of the world (2:2). The Son of God appeared to destroy the devil's work (3:8). John insists that it was through the human character of Jesus that people came to know the very nature of God's love: they know love because "Jesus Christ laid down his life for us" (3:16), and even more elaborately because "God showed his love for us by sending his only Son into the world that we might live through him. . . . [H]e loved us and sent his Son as an atoning sacrifice for our sins" (4:9–10). Clearly, for 1 John it was not only that Jesus was "God's Son" in an ontological sense that was critical, but that Jesus' own mode of self-donation was the very expression of God's love toward humans.

1 John makes it clear that learning Jesus means living in the world in the manner Jesus himself did. "The one who claims to remain in him must also walk in the way that he himself walked" (2:6). Followers must "believe in the name of his Son Jesus Christ and love one another just as he commanded us" (3:23). The letter also explicitly states that this cannot be a matter of mere verbal profession. True faith demands a moral transformation (1:15–17) and above all a sharing of the things needed for life with those who are needy. In 3:16, John says, "In this we have come to know love, because he laid down his life for us; we must also lay down our lives for the brethren." This statement is followed immediately by the assertion that such love cannot possibly dwell in one who, having the resources for physical life, refuses to share them with the needy (3:17), and then by this conclusion: "Little children, let us love not with word nor with speech but in deed and in truth" (3:18).

1 PETER

The author of this remarkable letter identifies himself as an "apostle of Jesus Christ" (1:1) and as a "witness to the sufferings of Christ" (5:1). There is no compelling reason to deny the possibility that Peter the disciple of Jesus was that author, even as there is no decisive way to demonstrate that he was. Authorship, in any case, is of little importance except as it pertains to the question of diversity and unity in the early church. Many scholars have remarked on the striking similarity in outlook between 1 Peter and many of the Pauline letters. This similarity is less likely to be due to a later Paulinist writing in the name of Peter than it is to be due to a certain range of shared convictions even within the diversity of expressions in early Christianity.

In terms of the present, 1 Peter designates Jesus as God's Son and as Lord (1:3). Jesus is resurrected from the dead (1:3), and that is his "glorification" (1:21). After his resurrection, he goes "in the Spirit" to preach to the souls in prison (2:19). His resurrection is described as going to heaven to be at God's right hand (3:22). He is now the one through whom spiritual sacrifices are offered to God (2:5), and God is praised through him (4:11). With respect to humans, the living Jesus is the "chief shepherd" (5:4). It is his resurrection that enables baptism to "save" people in the present (3:21). Because he shares in the power of God, Jesus will also be revealed in the future (1:7, 13). Believers have been called to eternal glory "in Christ" (5:10).

There is an equally rich perception of Jesus' humanity in 1 Peter. Jesus was "chosen before the foundation of the world, but appeared at the end of the ages for your sake" (1:20). Similarly contrasting language is used of Jesus' human existence: he was the stone rejected by the builders that became the cornerstone (2:8); he was put to death in the body and made alive in the Spirit (2:18). He suffered in his body (4:1), and the pattern of his first suffering and then entering glory was foretold by the prophets (1:11). His death is clearly understood as a sacrifice undertaken for the sake of others. Peter speaks of the "sprinkling of his blood" (1:2) and notes that Christians have been redeemed "by the precious blood of Christ, as a lamb without blemish or defect" (1:19). And again: "Christ died for sins once for all, the righteous for the unrighteous, to bring you to God" (3:18). Peter stresses not only the fact of Jesus' vicarious sacrifice but also the manner in which he endured its suffering. Thus in 2:22–25 Peter ascribes to Jesus the silent and patient suffering of the innocent victim prophesied in Isaiah 53:4–9. Jesus' *moral* attitude and character are an essential dimension to his self-giving life: "He committed no sin; no guile was found on his lips. When he was reviled, he did not revile in return; when he suffered, he did not threaten; but he trusted to him who judges justly. He himself bore our sins in his body on the tree" (2:22–24, RSV).

How does 1 Peter envisage the process of learning Jesus? That process involves in the first place "obedience to Jesus Christ" (1:2); followers are also to "reverence Christ in [their] hearts as Lord" (3:15). But Peter adds a dimension of relatedness that is distinctive—namely, that of love on the part of the believer. Speaking to Gentile converts, he says, "Without having seen him you love him, even though you do not now see him, you believe in him and exalt with unspeakable and exalted joy" (1:8). They come to learn Jesus above all by following in his path. Peter declares that Christ "suffered for your sake, leaving an example for you, so that you might follow in his steps" (2:21), and then describes the mode of Jesus' suffering in the manner of the suffering servant of Isaiah (2:22–24). To suffer in the manner Jesus did is not a mechanical imitation but an actual participation in the pattern of Jesus' existence: "But just as you share in the sufferings of Christ, rejoice, so that you might also exalt and be glad when his glory is revealed" (4:13). Just as Jesus moved through suffering to that glory which was a share in God's own life, so does the gift of the Holy Spirit from Jesus transform the meaning of the suffering of followers: "If you are reviled for the name of Christ, you are blessed, because the Spirit of glory and of God rests on you" (4:14).

LETTER TO THE HEBREWS

Not really a letter but rather a "word of exhortation" (13:22) addressed to Christians who—because of discouragement caused by social ostracism and the loss of their property on account of their allegiance to Christ (10:32–36)—are in danger of falling away from their first commitment (13:3–17), Hebrews is a masterpiece of rhetoric, one of the longest and most powerful theological arguments in the New Testament. At the heart of its argument is the figure of Jesus. In order to convince his readers to remain faithful, the author seeks to persuade them that in the life and death and new life of Jesus they have a better hope than any other that can be found (6:13–20).

The distinctive image for Jesus employed by Hebrews is that of the high priest (2:17; 3:2; 4:14–15; 5:10; 6:20; 7:1; 8:1, 11) who "makes atonement for the sins of the people" (2:17). As such, he is the "mediator of a superior covenant" (8:6; 9:13; 12:24) and the guarantor of a better covenant (7:22). Because Jesus is therefore the go-between for God and humans, Hebrews emphasizes both Jesus' derivation from God and his fully human roots. Thus Jesus is the "Son" of God (1:2, 3, 8; 3:6; 4:14; 7:1, 28; 10:29) and God's "apostle" (3:1) who "came into the world" (10:5). As a human, he shared completely in the experiences of humans (2:11–14), including testing (2:18; 4:15) and death (2:9). Yet God "brought back from the dead the Lord Jesus, the great shepherd of the sheep" (13:20), so that Jesus, having entered into heaven itself (9:24), sits at the right hand of God (10:12), where he lives forever (7:24). He now makes intercession for the people forever (7:25). Jesus Christ is therefore "the same yesterday, and today, and forever" (13:18), and through Jesus the community can offer to God its sacrifice of praise (13:13). Having dealt with sin in his first coming, Jesus will appear "to those who are expecting him for salvation" (9:27–28).

When Hebrews "sees Jesus," it sees one who "for a little while was made lower than the angels," but is now "crowned with glory and honor because of the suffering of death, so that by the grace of God he might taste death for everyone" (2:9, RSV). On the one hand, it is because Jesus shared "the very stamp of [God's] nature" that his humanity had such singular significance and his death had such effect: "By his death he might destroy him who holds the power of death" (2:14). It is also because he has been "perfected" and has entered into the life of God that Jesus can be both the "cause of eternal salvation to all who obey him" (5:9) and the Lord who "first spoke" such salvation (2:3).

On the other hand, no writing in the New Testament puts more emphasis on the human disposition of Jesus. He shared the lot of humans entirely (2:16) and was tested like all humans:

> For surely it is not with the angels that he is concerned but with the descendents of Abraham. Therefore he had to be made like his brethren in every respect, so that he might become a merciful and

faithful high priest in the service of God to make expiation for the sins of the people. For because he himself has suffered and been tempted, he is able to help those who are tempted. (2:16–18, RSV)

The difference between Jesus and the rest of humanity is that he did not sin (4:15). He is therefore able to "sympathize with our weaknesses" (4:15) even though, unlike us, he remained "faithful to the one who appointed him" (3:2). The prime example of Jesus' being tested and remaining faithful is given in 5:7–9. In an apparent allusion to a scene before Jesus' death that is also reported in the Synoptic Gospels (compare Mark 14:32–42, for example), Hebrews pictures Jesus "in the days of his flesh" praying not to experience death: "Jesus offered up prayers and supplications, with loud cries and tears, to him who was able to save him from death, and he was heard for his godly fear. Although he was a Son, he learned obedience through what he suffered" (5:7–8, RSV).

Hebrews perceives Jesus' experience of suffering as the means by which he was perfected in his humanity and therefore in his capacity to represent all humans before God (2:10): "Although he was a Son, he learned obedience through what he suffered" (5:8). Although he "came into the world" (10:5) with the express intention "to do your will, O God" (10:7–9), Jesus had to learn through the experience of testing what obedience truly was, and he expressed his obedience most perfectly in his death on the cross: "Through that will we have been made holy through the sacrifice of the body of Jesus Christ once for all" (10:10).

Jesus is high priest because in his death he offered himself as a means of atonement between humans and God: He sacrificed for their sins "once for all when he offered himself" (7:27), and "he appeared once for all at the end of the ages to put away sin by the offering of himself" (9:26). It was both his own will and "his own blood" (8:12) that were offered on behalf of others; he went into the sanctuary on our behalf (6:20), passing through the veil that was his own flesh (10:20) into the eternal presence of God:

". . . the blood of Christ who offered himself through the eternal Spirit . . . so that we may serve the living God" (9:13–14). Because of his resurrection and enthronement in the presence of God, the effect of his sacrifice is eternal. His "sprinkled blood speaks better than the blood of Abel" (12:24).

For the author of Hebrews, Jesus' death for others is also the perfect expression of his fidelity to God. The humanity of Jesus and the character of his human will are significant precisely because in his humanity he has shown "the new and living way" (10:20) into the presence of God. Jesus is therefore the "pioneer and perfecter of faith, who for the joy that was set before him endured the cross, despising the shame, and is seated at the right hand of the throne of God" (12:2, RSV). Jesus' death was shameful in human eyes: he "endured hostility from sinners" (12:3) and was crucified (6:6) outside the city, suffering "outside the gate in order to sanctify the people through his own blood" (13:12). For those who associate themselves with Jesus, it is necessary to follow in the same path of faith, with its attendant suffering: "Let us therefore go toward him outside the camp and bear the reviling he endured" (13:13). Those who turn away after having "tasted the heavenly gift and [having] become partakers of the Holy Spirit," accepting the measure of the world rather than the measure of Jesus' faith for their lives, "crucify the Son of God for themselves and hold him up to contempt" (6:4–6).

Diverse Witnesses, Same Person

Each of these early Christian writings—a full third of the New Testament canon!—has its own distinctive perspective and purpose. It is impossible to harmonize them on every issue. They point to some of the rich diversity of experience and conviction in the first generation of the Christian movement. Even concerning Jesus, we find in them considerable variation. One does not mention Jesus at all (3 John) and another only twice (James), while others mention Jesus too often for easy summation (1 Peter, 1 John,

Hebrews). We can see also that some titles and images dominate in certain writings and occur infrequently or not at all in others.

Yet for all this variety, the understanding of Jesus is remarkably stable. Jesus is perceived first of all in terms of his present power and his relationship to God, as well as in terms of his future coming as judge and Savior. Jesus' humanity, however, is by no means neglected. In addition to giving the incidental facts of his human existence—that he was of the children of Abraham and the tribe of Judah, was born of a woman, was transfigured on the mountain, was tested before his death, bore witness before rulers—these texts give surprising attention to Jesus' words: not only those spoken through prophecy in the Spirit that find their way into the Gospel tradition (see Rev. 3:3, 20) and those that we know from the Synoptics that we can recognize recontextualized (see James 2:5–8), but also Jesus' "declaration" (Heb. 2:3) and "commandment" (2 Pet. 3:9), and "promise" (2 Pet. 3:2) all of which remain authoritative for the church. Most of all, Jesus' humanity is important because of his death—not simply the fact of his suffering but the manner of it: first, that his death was a sacrifice in blood in order to bring life and sanctification to others; second, that his death was willingly suffered for others by an innocent and righteous person.

These writings also make it clear that the "learning of Jesus" is more than a matter of formal confession. Learning Jesus also means living according to his words and by the measure of his faith. It means continuing to bear witness in the world to the reality of God as Jesus bore witness. It means walking in the path of suffering for others that he himself followed. The Jesus learned in these compositions is a Jesus who by his resurrection is the source of eternal life and by his suffering and death is the model for obedient faith in God.

CHAPTER 6

Paul's Witness to Jesus

The letters attributed to the Apostle Paul would seem to have obvious importance for learning Jesus. Paul's importance as a missionary in the first generation after the death of Jesus is confirmed by the narrative role assigned him by the Acts of the Apostles. His letters are the earliest datable witnesses to the meaning of Jesus for Christians in that first generation.

Yet for many, Paul's witness is uncertain and suspect. *Uncertain* because of the opinion that not all the letters attributed to Paul in the canon actually came from him. Many scholars accept only seven letters as authentic (Romans, 1 and 2 Corinthians, 1 Thessalonians, Galatians, Philemon, and Philippians). This means that the other six letters (2 Thessalonians, Colossians, Ephesians, 1 Timothy, 2 Timothy, and Titus) might have been written by other writers associating themselves with Paul's authority after his death. *Suspect* because of the opinion that Paul had little interest in Jesus as such and was indeed primarily responsible for transforming the "Jesus movement" into the "Christ cult"—and by so doing began the process by which the "real Jesus" was suppressed by the tyranny of the creed.

The reasons for thinking Paul did not write all the letters attributed to him are not particularly convincing: given the manifest variety even within the undisputed letters, the degree of variation demonstrated by each of the disputed compositions is not so severe as to demand a conclusion of nonauthenticity. No one, in any case, disputes that the thirteen letters attributed to Paul in the canon represent (each in its own fashion) a distinctively Pauline perspective. In this chapter, I will treat them all as part of "Paul's witness to Jesus." It is with considerable reluctance that I do *any* grouping, however, since I am committed to the principle that each New Testament composition should be read on its own terms. Only the strictures of space justify the compression and abstraction that inevitably result from treating the letters as a whole rather than individually.

Concerning Paul's putative disinterest in the human Jesus in favor of a mythic Christ, the evidence must be allowed to speak. We have already seen evidence sufficient to counter the opinion that Paul alone is responsible for a fundamental reinterpretation of Jesus. Even if 1 Peter and Hebrews could be taken to represent "Pauline" positions, it is impossible to claim that any of the three letters of John or Revelation or 2 Peter or Jude is part of Pauline Christianity. Yet in all of these writings we have found Jesus to be understood primarily from the perspective of his resurrection and present power in the church; his humanity has been appreciated above all for the significance of his death as loving self-donation and as a sacrifice for the sins of others. If these same emphases appear in Paul's letters, it is more likely because he shared in a common Christian understanding than because his personal inventions subverted and then suppressed other understandings.

The Living Lord

Jesus is for Paul preeminently "the Lord," the one whom he encountered—or better, the one who encountered him—as the Son of God in power and changed him in an instant from the persecutor of the church to an apostle sent out to proclaim Jesus as Messiah and Lord to all nations (Gal. 1:15–16; 1 Cor. 9:1; 15:8–11; 1 Tim. 1:12–17). There is no evidence that Paul knew Jesus before his death—or even knew of him. When Paul speaks of "once regarding Jesus according to the flesh" (2 Cor. 5:16), he is referring not to any knowledge he had of Jesus during Jesus' lifetime but rather to the perspective he had on Jesus when he first encountered him as the crucified (absent) leader of the "Jesus movement." Paul was a persecutor of Christians not because of personal acquaintance with Jesus but because, as one zealous for Torah (Gal. 1:13–14), he regarded the Christian claim that Jesus was a resurrected Messiah to be blasphemous. Paul had no doubt that Jesus could not be the Holy One because, according to Torah, his manner of death was as one cursed by God: "Cursed be every one who hangs upon a tree" (Deut. 21:23; see Gal. 3:13). But then Paul encountered the risen Jesus and was called by him to be an apostle: "Last of all he appeared also to me" (1 Cor. 15:8). Paul connects his role as an apostle precisely to this experience: "Am I not free? Am I not an apostle? Have I not seen Jesus our Lord?" (1 Cor. 9:1, RSV). Paul's perspective is now radically altered, and he "knows [Jesus] that way no longer" (2 Cor. 5:16).

How does Paul perceive Jesus? After his encounter with him, Paul certainly thinks of Jesus as the Jewish Messiah, despite his earlier conviction to the contrary. This is so much the case that in his letters the title "Messiah" *(Christos)* is often used as if it were part of Jesus' name. And in other places, the title "Messiah" appears by itself even without Jesus' personal name (see especially Rom. 9–11). But in Paul's eyes, Jesus is also much more than a divinely anointed figure within Judaism. If Jesus were simply the foretold Messiah, his relevance might well be limited to the Jewish people; yet Paul calls the early church to proclaim Jesus to all nations, showing that he perceives Jesus as having significance beyond Israel.

This significance is based not so much on Jesus' life within Judaism as on Jesus' new life in the Spirit, beginning with his resurrection from the dead. If the resurrection of Jesus is a "new creation" (2 Cor. 5:17), and Jesus is the "first fruits of those who have fallen asleep" in his resurrection (1 Cor. 15:20), then Jesus can be understood as a "new Adam," the start of a new humanity. His significance is therefore for all humans, Gentiles as well as Jews. The first Adam was simply a living being (1 Cor. 15:45) whose sin brought death into the world (Rom. 5:12). Jesus as the new Adam became life-giving Spirit (1 Cor. 15:45), and his righteousness brought the possibility of eternal life—that is, a share in God's own life—to all the world:

If because of one man's trespass, death reigned through that one man, much more will those who receive the abundance of grace and the free gift of righteousness reign in life through the one man Jesus Christ. Then as one man's trespass led to condemnation for all men, so one man's act of righteousness leads to acquittal and life for all men. For as by one man's disobedience many were made sinners, so by one man's obedience many will be made righteous. (Rom. 5: 17–19, RSV)

For Paul, Jesus was "God's Son" who was sent into the world (Gal. 4:4), but he was established as "Son of God in power" by virtue of the resurrection (Rom. 1:4). Through the act of being raised from the dead, Jesus entered into God's own life and God's own power. He is therefore best named "Lord" *(Kyrios)*. The title *Kyrios* is God's own name in the Septuagint translation of Torah's word *Yahweh* (LXX Exod. 3:2–15). Jesus is given this title since he rules over all creation with the very power of God (Phil. 2:10–11; Col. 1:15–20). To be "in Christ," for Paul, means also to be "in the Lord"—that is, to have the Holy Spirit, which enables one to confess that "Jesus is Lord" (1 Cor. 12:1–3). To hold any other perspective on Jesus than that which declares him to have such life and such power is to see him "according to the flesh," and therefore in a real sense to "curse Jesus" (1 Cor. 12:3). To hold any other perspective means to see Jesus not as the source of God's blessing but as one who because of his manner of death is separated from God by curse (Gal. 3:13): "I want you to understand that no one speaking by the Spirit of God says, 'Jesus be cursed!' and no one is able to say, 'Jesus is Lord!' except by the Holy Spirit" (1 Cor. 12:3).

Paul develops three corollaries from these convictions concerning Jesus' resurrection life. The first is that Jesus' presence and power are only partially manifested in the signs and wonders worked in the church and are not yet fully established on the plane of human experience and history (1

Thess. 4:13–5:10). The triumph that God has accomplished in Christ is in that sense "hidden," not yet fully revealed (Col. 3:1 4). Jesus will partici-pate in a future victory of God over both sin and death (1 Cor. 15:20–28, 51–57), and "on that day" he will function as judge of the living and the dead to reckon to each person according to each one's deeds (Rom. 2:16; 2 Tim. 4:1).

The second corollary is the obverse of the first: God's victory in the resurrection of Jesus *is* present powerfully among those who have been gifted by the Holy Spirit (Rom. 8:1–27; 15:19; Gal. 3:3–5; 1 Thess. 1:5; 1 Cor. 12:4–11; 2 Cor. 3:17–18). The resurrection of Jesus is not something that happened to him alone; it has cosmic significance that now shows it-self primarily in the powerful transformative effects of the Holy Spirit and will only later become obvious to all (Rom. 8:18–25). Because those who have "drunk the Spirit" (1 Cor. 12:13) also "live by the Spirit" (Gal. 5:25), they can also "walk by the Spirit" (Gal. 5:25) in newness of life (Rom. 6:4; 7:6). Paul draws an extraordinarily close relationship between what God accomplished in the death and resurrection of Jesus and what God is doing in those who have been given the Spirit of Jesus: what happened in Jesus is also to happen—in fact, is already happening—in them (Rom. 8:9–15; 1 Thess. 4:14). The life they now lead is not simply their own but that of "Christ who lives in [them]" (Gal. 2:20).

The third corollary is that the truth about Jesus as God's son is deter-mined from the life of God that he now shares. That Jesus' humanity is now capable of sharing God's life by resurrection, for example, suggests also that—at least in some fashion—this status was his even before his birth as human: Jesus' "being in the form of God" was something that could be emptied out by taking on humanity (Phil. 2:6), just as something rich can be exchanged for poverty (2 Cor. 8:9), something powerful can be ex-changed for weakness (1 Cor. 1:21–25; 2 Cor. 13:4), and something righ-teous can be exchanged for sin (2 Cor. 5:21).

Likewise, if Jesus is now the one "through whom" life now comes to humans, does it not follow that he has a similar function in God's creative work (1 Cor. 8:6)? If Jesus is the head of the church, is there not a sense in which he is also head of creation (Col. 1:15–20)? If Jesus is the source of the "supernatural food and supernatural drink" shared by believers on the "Lord's day" meal (1 Cor. 10:14–22), does it not make sense to see Jesus as in some sense also proleptically present in God's activities described in Torah? Thus Paul can say that the gospel of Jesus Christ was "promised ahead of time in the prophets" (Rom. 1:2–3) and that the words of Torah speak directly of Christ (Rom. 10:5–9; 1 Cor. 10:1–4).

Paul's appreciation of Jesus' present and future is so pervasive and richly developed that it is virtually impossible to summarize. Look at what he says in statements about "Jesus" (leaving aside other titles) in the shortest and longest of his letters. The Letter to Philemon has a mere twenty-five verses, but in them we learn that Jesus is the Lord in whom believers have faith (5), that it is in his service that Paul is a prisoner (1, 9, 22), and that he is the source of grace and peace (3, 25). The Letter to the Romans, in contrast, has sixteen chapters. In Romans, we find Jesus also designated as Lord repeatedly and in many connections: as the one Paul serves as a slave (1:1), as the source of grace and peace (1:7; 5:1; 16:20, 24), as the one God raised from the dead (4:24) and confessed as such for salvation (10:9), and as the one in whom humans will reign (5:21) and in whom those who are made righteous make their boast (5:11, 17). Christians are baptized into Jesus (6:3), and in him they now have no condemnation (8:1); in him also they are living to God (6:11) and have the eternal life (6:23) that comes from the Spirit of life (8:2)—namely, the Spirit of the one who raised Jesus from the dead (8:11).

We learn also in Romans that God is the father of Jesus (15:6), that people belong to Jesus (1:6), have confidence in (14:14) and possess the love of God in Jesus (8:39), and can even "put on the Lord Jesus Christ" (13:14). It is through Jesus that exhortations are made to the readers (15:30) and through Jesus that prayers are offered to God (1:8; 7:25; 16:27).

In the future God will judge all humans through Jesus (2:16), and through Jesus believers will "reign in life" (5:17).

Paul's letters, in short—like all the other early Christian literature we have surveyed—portray Jesus primarily not as a figure of the past but as a figure of the present and of the future.

The Humanity of Jesus

At one level, Paul's language about Jesus can appropriately be called mythic. Indeed, it is downright impossible to talk about a human person bearing divine power *without* using myth. When Paul declares that "God was in Christ reconciling the world to himself" (2 Cor. 5:19), he is stating a reality that transcends the realm of ordinary history and the categories of historiography.

Although Paul's language is necessarily mythic insofar as it seeks to express a significance beyond the empirical, Paul's Jesus is by no means simply a "mythic figure." Jesus is not an otherworldly visitor, or a phantom divine presence masquerading as human. In Paul's letters, the humanity of Jesus is real and specific.

These letters contain a surprising amount of factual information about Jesus—*surprising* because of the emphasis Paul places on the present and future significance of Jesus as Lord. Paul does not retell stories about Jesus, and thus his factual references are scattered and out of sequence. If we did not have the Gospel narratives, we probably would not know in what order those references should be placed. Yet the same sentence that begins with one of Paul's most "mythic" statements—namely, "In the fullness of time God sent his son"—continues, "born of a woman, born under the law" (Gal. 4:4). For Paul, Jesus was human, and he was Jewish. Furthermore, he came "to redeem those who were under the law" (Gal. 4:5); in other words, his human mission was first of all to his fellow Jews. Similarly, Paul states in Romans 15:7 that "Christ became a minister of circumcision to show God's truthfulness." Jesus was not only Jewish; he had a specific Jewish heritage—"descended from David according to the flesh" (Rom. 1:3; see also 2 Tim. 2:8, "descended from David according to my gospel")—and ministry.

Paul knows that Jesus taught, for he refers to "the word of the Lord" (1 Thess. 4:15) and "a charge of the Lord" (1 Cor. 7:10) and "the command of the Lord" (1 Cor. 9:14). Because of the way he connects adoption as sons of God to the Aramaic cry of "Abba, Father" (Gal. 4:6; see Rom. 8:15), it is likely that he was familiar with a tradition holding that this was Jesus' distinctive way of addressing God (see Mark 14:36). Paul knows that Jesus shared a meal "on the night he was betrayed [or arrested]" (1 Cor. 11:23), and he connects the death of Jesus to the Passover (1 Cor. 5:7).

Paul places the death of Jesus in Judea (1 Thess. 2:14) and blames it on the Jews, "who killed the Lord Jesus and the prophets" (1 Thess. 4:15). But he also blames earthly rulers: "None of the rulers of this age knew, for if they had known they would not have crucified the Lord of glory" (1 Cor. 2:8). In 1 Timothy 6:13, he is more precise: "Christ Jesus . . . in his testimony before Pontius Pilate made the good confession." Paul obviously knows that Jesus was crucified (1 Cor. 2:2; Gal. 3:1; Phil. 2:8), and he knows the tradition of Jesus' burial (1 Cor. 15:4) and of appearances after his death to Cephas, James, the Twelve, five hundred at one time, and James, before he also appeared to Paul himself (1 Cor. 15:7).

This is no small fund of information about the life and death of Jesus. Paul's letters, in fact, are the most comprehensive and reliable source of factual information—apart from the Gospels themselves—about the human Jesus.

Paul also adds to our knowledge about the sayings of Jesus. Although he does not refer to these sayings often, when he does he treats them as authoritative. In 1 Thessalonians 4:15, he does not directly cite Jesus when he refers to a "word of the Lord," but the content of his subsequent assertion concerning the "coming of the Lord" makes it likely that he is referring to an eschatological saying of Jesus such as is found in Matthew 24:30–31 and Mark 13:26–27. Similarly, in 1 Corinthians 9:14, he says, "In the same way the Lord commanded that those who proclaim the gospel should get their living from the gospel," an apparent allusion to a saying that is now found in Luke 10:7. And in 1 Timothy 5:18 that saying is quoted directly: "The laborer deserves his wages." When Paul says in 1 Corinthians 7:10–11, "To the married I give charge, not I but the Lord, that the wife should not separate from the husband (but if she does let her remain single or else be reconciled to her husband)—and that the husband should not divorce his wife," he is clearly referring to the saying of Jesus as found in Mark 10:2–9.

The clearest and longest citation from the words of Jesus is found in a narrative fragment cited by Paul in 1 Corinthians 11:23–25 (see also Matt. 26:26–29; Mark 14:22–25; Luke 22:14–20):

> [T]he Lord Jesus on the night he was betrayed took bread, and when he had given thanks he broke it, and said, "This is my body which is for you. Do this in remembrance of me." In the same way also the cup, after supper, saying, "This cup is the new covenant in my blood. Do this, as often as you drink it, in remembrance of me."

On the basis of these words, Paul rebukes the Corinthians for their misbehavior at the Lord's Supper (1 Cor. 11:26–32, RSV).

It is not certain how large a collection of Jesus' sayings Paul might have had. We are puzzled, for example, that in 1 Corinthians 8–10, when Paul at considerable length discusses eating meat that had been offered to idols, he does not make use of Jesus' explicit statement found in Mark 7:15: "There is nothing outside a person which by going into him can defile him; but the things which come out of a person are what defile him." Perhaps Paul did not have this memory of Jesus, which would not be surprising in the period of oral tradition during which Paul was writing his letters. It would be highly unlikely, in fact, for all of Jesus' sayings to be in the possession of every community or every teacher. What is obvious is that when Paul *does* quote Jesus, he quotes him as "Lord"—that is, as present and living authority whose words direct behavior.

It is Jesus' final act in death that has the greatest significance for Paul. I use the expression "act in death" deliberately, for although Paul uses traditional language concerning Jesus' death as a "sacrifice in blood" (Rom. 3:25; 5:9; Eph. 1:7; 2:13; Col. 1:20), as do the authors of several of the other New Testament compositions we have surveyed (Revelation, 1 John, 1 Peter, Hebrews), his language does not suggest the mechanical offering of a body but rather the free self-disposition of a human person. Thus, in the passage where Paul most clearly describes Jesus' death as an "expiation," he combines the terms "in his blood" and "through faith" so that they make a single reality (Rom. 3:25). God's righteousness is revealed, says Paul, through the faith of Jesus Christ (Rom. 3:22), a righteousness that can justify those who "are out of the faith of Jesus" (Rom. 3:26).

For Paul, therefore, what is most significant about the human Jesus is not the facts about his life or the words he spoke but the character of his response to God. What does Paul mean by the "faith of Jesus"? We take a clue from the fact that he speaks about the "obedience of faith" (Rom. 1:5; 16:25) in a way that makes the two terms interpret each other. In Romans 5:12–21, for example, we find that the "faith of Jesus" is explicated precisely in terms of the "obedience of the one man Jesus" in contrast to the disobedience of the one man Adam. Jesus' faith is his trusting fidelity and obedience to God. It is in this way that he is truly the "seed of Abraham" (Gal. 3:16). And because he is "God's Son" and the new Adam, his "yes" to God is of critical importance to all those humans of whom he is the "first-born":

> For the son of God, Jesus Christ, whom we preached among
> you, Silvanus and Timothy and I, was not Yes and No; but in him it

is always Yes. For all the promises of God find their Yes in him. That is why we utter the Amen through him, to the glory of God. (2 Cor. 1:19–20, RSV)

Paul spells out the significance of Jesus' obedience most fully in Philippians 2:5–11. That passage makes it clear first that Jesus' death on the cross was the final expression of an obedience to God that characterized his entire human existence and second that his "yes" to God was answered by God's "yes" to him in Jesus' exaltation:

> Though he was in the form of God [he] did not count equality with God a thing to be grasped, but emptied himself, taking the form of a servant, being born in the likeness of men. And being found in human form, he humbled himself and became obedient unto death, even death on a cross. Therefore God has highly exalted him and has bestowed on him the name which is above every name, that at the name of Jesus every knee should bow, in heaven and earth and under the earth, and every tongue confess that Jesus is Lord, to the glory of God the Father. (RSV)

There is still another aspect of Jesus' human character that Paul makes explicit—namely, his love for others. In Romans 5:6–8, Paul seeks to express what the death of Jesus means in terms of human experience:

> While we were still weak, at the right time, Christ died for the ungodly. Someone will scarcely die for a righteous person—though perhaps one will dare even to die for the good. But God shows his own love for us in that while we were still sinners, Christ died for us.

Paul regards this demonstration of God's love also as a manifestation of Jesus' personal and human love toward others. In Galatians 1:3–4, he refers to "our Lord Jesus Christ who gave himself for our sins to deliver us from the present evil age," and in Galatians 2:20 he asserts that "the life I now live I live by the faith of the son of God, who loved me and gave himself for me." In Ephesians 5:2, likewise, Paul tells his readers, "Walk in love, as Christ also loved us and gave himself up for us, a fragrant offering and sacrifice to God." Finally, in Titus 2:14, he speaks of "Jesus Christ, who gave himself for us to redeem us from all lawlessness." When Paul refers to "the grace of God and the free gift in the grace of that one man Jesus Christ" (Rom. 5:15), then, he means not only that Jesus is the gift God gave to humans, but that the human person Jesus was self-donative, giving himself to others as an expression of love.

The Mind of Christ and the Story of Jesus

For Paul, "learning Jesus" means more than gaining information about a person who lived in the past. It means participating in a spiritual transformation in the image of Jesus leading to a life conformed to the pattern of Jesus' own human character. Thus, to make clear the contrast between their new way of living and that of the Gentile world—of which they were once a part—Paul tells the Ephesians, "You did not so learn the Messiah!—if indeed you have heard about him and were taught in him as the truth is in Jesus." And what does this mean? "Put off your old nature which belongs to your former manner of life and is corrupt through deceitful lusts, and be renewed in the spirit of your minds, and put on the new nature, created after the likeness of God in true righteousness and holiness" (Eph. 4:20–24, RSV).

For Paul, the Holy Spirit is not an external force but an internal power that can reach and transform human freedom:

> Now the Lord is the Spirit. And where the Spirit of the Lord is there is freedom. And we all, with unveiled faces, beholding the glory of the Lord, are being changed into his likeness from one degree of glory to another; for this comes from the Lord who is Spirit. (2 Cor. 3:17–18, RSV)

The intimacy among the Holy Spirit, the risen Jesus, and the believer could not be greater, in Paul's view. The Holy Spirit empowers and enables a new way of life fashioned according to the image of the one who is its source, Jesus, who by resurrection became "life-giving Spirit" (1 Cor. 15:45): "Just as we have borne the image of the man of dust, so shall we also bear the image of the man of heaven" (1 Cor. 15:49). The means by which this "image of Christ" is impressed upon believers is the "renewal of their mind" (Rom. 12:2), so that they perceive reality and respond to it according to the "mind of Christ" (1 Cor. 2:16). They "put on the Lord Jesus Christ" (Rom. 13:14):

> You have put off the old nature with its practices and have put on the new nature which is being renewed in knowledge after the image of its creator. Here there cannot be Greek and Jew, circumcised and uncircumcised, barbarian, Scythian, slave, free person, but Christ is all, and in all. (Col. 3:9–11, RSV)

Paul makes his most explicit use of the story of Jesus in connection with living according to the "mind of Christ." He does not refer to Jesus' sayings or deeds but evokes and alludes to the basic *pattern* of Jesus' behavior that reveals his character as human and his identity as Messiah. Thus in Galatians 6:2 Paul tells his readers, "Bear one another's burdens and so fulfill the law of Christ." The *nomos Christou* (perhaps better translated not "law of Christ" but "pattern of the Messiah") is filled out by a mode of life that seeks the good of the other even at cost to oneself: bearing one another's burdens. The story of Jesus is the norm for the moral character of the community.

Paul's distinctive insight is that the *particulars* of Jesus' historical existence are simply past and in some sense irrelevant. It is the *pattern* of Jesus' story that the Spirit can reshape, again and again, in countless lives; the *image* of Jesus that can be formed in all humans with that freedom that comes from the Lord who is Spirit. This does not make the humanity of

Jesus less but more significant, for the *way* Jesus was human—the way he responded to God in faithful obedience and gave his life in service to other humans—is the pattern for all authentic humanity renewed by the Spirit of God.

In 1 Corinthians, for example, Paul sees *nous Christou* ("the mind of Christ") as an understanding that is measured not by the "wisdom of the world" but by the "wisdom of the cross." He means by this a sense of how the gifts of the Spirit can appropriately be used to build the community as the "body of the Messiah" (see 1 Cor. 1:18–2:16), according to the measure of a Messiah whose mission was spelled out in terms of shameful death:

> We preach a crucified Messiah, a stumbling block to Jews and folly to Gentiles, but to those who have been called, both Jews and Greeks, a Messiah who is the power of God and the wisdom of God. For the foolishness of God is wiser than men, and the weakness of God is stronger than men. (1 Cor. 1:23–25)

Paul's discussion of eating foods offered to idols in chapters 8–10 of 1 Corinthians shows how the "mind of Christ" is applied to specific circumstances. Although Paul recognizes people's right to follow their own conscience, he also asks them to relativize that right when the good of another is involved. Someone insisting on the right to eat at the risk of shaking the faith of a fellow member of the community is misusing that right: "And so by your knowledge this weak person is destroyed, the brother for whom Christ died. Thus sinning against your brethren and wounding their conscience when it is weak, you sin against Christ" (1 Cor. 8:11, RSV). Paul assumes a real connection between the story of Jesus and the behavior of the community. The phrase "the brother for whom Christ died" is a brief story fragment, alluding to a pattern in the story of Jesus that Paul could assume his readers would know and recognize in such cryptic form. The death of Jesus for the members of the community establishes a pattern of moral behavior between them as well as a connection to Jesus himself: when a brother's faith is destroyed, those in the community "sin against Christ" (1 Cor. 8:12).

In an earlier chapter I touched on the way Paul uses the pattern of Jesus' death for others in 1 Corinthians 11:17–32. It is worth repeating here. Paul upbraids the church for its behavior at the common meal: "Do you despise the church of God and humiliate those who have nothing?" In response, Paul cites the words of Jesus "on the night he was betrayed" (11:23). After quoting the words of Jesus over the bread and wine—the bread is his body "which is for you," and the wine is the blood "of the new covenant" (11:25)—Paul applies this critical part of Jesus' story to his community's behavior: "Whoever therefore eats the bread or drinks the cup of the Lord in an unworthy manner will be guilty of profaning the body and blood of the Lord" (11:27, RSV). By "unworthy manner" Paul means their eating and drinking "without discerning the body" that is the church (11:29)—that is, their scorning the needy and humiliating them. Paul here draws together the symbols of the community's meal to shape its moral character: followers of Jesus are to learn from the meal-memory of Jesus how to act toward each other. The one who "gave his body" for others is the model for a manner of life that "builds up the body" of the community (see 12:12, 27).

In Romans 13:14, Paul tells readers to "put on the Lord Jesus" and not gratify their selfish desires. He spells this out in his discussion of disputes over eating and other practices in the community. The norm for Christian behavior should be the building up of each other's faith: "If your brother is being caused sorrow by what you eat, you are no longer walking in love. Do not let what you eat cause the ruin of one for whom Christ died" (Rom. 14:15). The similarity to 1 Corinthians 8:11 is patent. In both cases, the death of Jesus is understood as an act of love that is a model for others. If people act contrary to this measure, they are "no longer walking in love." Paul goes on to say that the strong should bear with the weak rather than seeking to please themselves. The example of Jesus is again given as the reason: "For Christ did not please himself; but, as it is written, 'The revilings of those who revile you fell on me'" (Rom. 15:1–3; see LXX Ps. 68:10). Then Paul invokes the entire pattern of Jesus' work as Messiah as he exhorts his readers, "Welcome one another, then, as Christ has welcomed you, for the glory of God" (Rom. 15:7, RSV). A similar appeal to the human character of Jesus is found in 2 Corinthians 10:1, when Paul entreats the Corinthians "by the meekness and gentleness of Christ."

The most obvious instance of Paul using the story of Jesus as the model for a community's behavior is found in Philippians 2:1–11. Paul tells a community shaken by rivalry and envy to "have this mind among yourselves which is in Christ Jesus" (Phil. 2:5), precisely to illustrate how their sharing in the Spirit ought to lead them to seek each other's interests and not merely their own (2:1–4). The so-called Christ hymn of 2:6–11 shows Jesus not clinging to what was his by right but giving it up, out of obedience, in service to God. The way that Jesus thought is to be the way that they think within the community.

Ephesians provides a final example of how Paul uses the story of Jesus as paradigm for Christian discipleship. In 4:17–19, Paul warns readers not to live in the way of the Gentiles, for "you did not so learn Christ—if indeed you have heard of him and were taught in him *as the truth is in Jesus*" (4:20–21, emphasis added). The use of the personal name is striking, as is the suggestion that the way to learn the Messiah is according to the "truth that is in Jesus." Paul applies this pattern immediately in 4:32: "Be kind toward each other, tenderhearted, forgiving one another, as God in Christ forgave you." At first this may appear to be a theological proposition, but 5:2 shows that Paul is alluding to the story of Jesus: "Walk in love as Christ loved us and gave himself up for us, a fragrant offering and sacrifice to God." Jesus' obedient self-sacrifice is an act of love for others that forms the pattern for relations within the community.

It is astonishing that anyone should ever have suggested that Jesus was not important to Paul. His letters contain a rich and complex image of Jesus. As present and powerful Lord, Jesus is the source of the life-giving Spirit. And in the character of his human life, he is the very model of how humans are to think and act. The measure of Christian identity for Paul, as for the other authors whose writings we have reviewed, is "as the truth is in Jesus."

PART 2

Jesus in the Gospels

CHAPTER 7

One Person in Four Portraits

As living Spirit, Jesus finds embodiment in multiple forms, including the texts that speak of him in the New Testament (and in some fashion in the Old Testament as well). When Christians read the New Testament, they do so in the expectation of encountering Jesus. They seek not a Jesus hidden behind the texts but a Jesus revealed within the texts.

The images of Jesus in the Book of Revelation and the epistolary literature of the New Testament, as we have seen, are indeed complex. Each writing is a witness to Jesus as present and future Lord and as the human person whose attitudes and actions are the normative measure for life in communities that bear his name. Because each of these writings is human, it is also necessarily partial and inadequate in its witnessing. Yet while each is limited by its perspective, each is also precious precisely because of that particularity of vantage point. None contains Jesus entirely, yet none can be dismissed as irrelevant or unimportant. Readers know that the embodied image of Jesus emerges from reading and living with each of these witnesses.

In contrast to the writings whose explicit interest is in the shaping of Christian identity in the present and in which the story of Jesus remains mostly implicit, the four canonical Gospels are distinguished by their explicit attention to the story of Jesus in the past. For them, the concern for shaping Christian identity is just as real, but it is fitted within narratives in which Jesus plays the main role.

Despite this basic contrast, the Gospels resemble the other New Testament literature in several respects. First, they view the story of Jesus' past from the vantage point of the resurrection experience and conviction. They were composed not by neutral observers but by disciples committed to

Jesus as Lord, and this faith perspective colors every memory of Jesus contained in the narratives. Second, each Gospel's specific selection and shaping of community memories of Jesus is affected by its author's perception of the readers' situation. Third, the image of Jesus in each Gospel is distinct, though the varied portraits are recognizably of the same figure.

Resistance to Multiplicity

Many Christians, both ancient and modern, have resisted the obvious diversity of portraits of Jesus, especially in the Gospels, and have tried in several ways to deny, suppress, or overcome it. For some reason, the diversity of images of Jesus that is taken for granted in the other New Testament writings is regarded as a major problem in the Gospels. Why is this? Is it because the Gospels are narratives about a character in the past? Is it because most people think that in narratives there are only two options—namely, "history" and "legend"? Is it because "truth" is attached solely to that which is "historical"? The answer to all three questions is yes. But something else is also at work.

Since the first Greek philosophers, thinkers in the West have favored the single over the multiple. Pre-Socratic thinkers tried to find some unifying principle of being behind all diverse appearances. Plato carried the tendency to its logical extreme by declaring that truth could be found only in the one; concerning the many there could only be opinions. Truth must be one: that premise continues to exercise a powerful influence, above all when "truth" is understood referentially—that is, as an exact fit between a proposition and something to which the proposition refers.

As we saw in an earlier chapter, the second-century teacher Tatian found the multiplicity of the traditional Gospels a scandal, and he sought to remove it by composing the *Diatesseron*, a single narrative about Jesus woven from the four canonical Gospels. Marcion likewise thought that if the Gospels diverged theologically, only one of them could be correct; so he included his own expurgated version of the Gospel of Luke in his truncated canon, together with ten of Paul's letters, rejecting the other three canonical gospels as falsifications of Jesus' message

Only one can be true. Truth can be found only in the singular. In a benign form, the same premise lies behind the construction of all "Gospel harmonies," for as the very name indicates, they seek to dissolve multiplicity by resolving differences.

At a more naive level, the identical premise governs the dismayed question of the young college or seminary student confronted for the first time with discrepancies between the various accounts of Jesus' acts and words: "But which of them is true?" What that question means is, "Which of them corresponds with what happened?"

The question assumes that the Gospels intend to report facts, and that "truth" is a simple correspondence between the facts and the report. If there is more than one account and the accounts differ in fundamental ways (so this logic goes), either one of them must be true and the others false, or they all must be false. Again, the truth must be singular, not plural.

At a more sophisticated level, this is the reasoning that dominated the first "quest for the historical Jesus," which was in essence a search for the one Gospel source that would prove to be an accurate report concerning Jesus. Since John was so dramatically different from the Synoptic Gospels (Matthew, Mark, and Luke) on so many counts, it was quickly dismissed as "untrue"—that is, as unreliable concerning the facts about Jesus. Efforts to solve the "Synoptic problem"—in other words, to ascertain the sequence of dependence between Matthew, Mark, and Luke—were likewise in service of determining the earliest and (it was presumed) most reliable source for the facts about Jesus.

Mark was eventually considered by the majority of critical scholars to be the least affected by later faith perspectives, and therefore most "true" as a historical source. But when Mark in turn also came to be perceived as "interpretation" rather than "report," the first quest ended in a state of skepticism concerning the ability to find a historical Jesus.

In the recently renewed quest for the historical Jesus, a similar premise has generated still another attempt to eliminate the plurality of the Gospels. But this time the characteristic of the Gospels that has made them most valuable to centuries of believers—namely, their witness and interpretation of Jesus in light of his resurrection—is being regarded as a fatal disqualification from "historical truth." Only bits and pieces of "authentic" sayings and deeds can be excavated from those literary narratives—pulled out from behind the living memories of those who believed in him—and made available for a new reconstruction of who Jesus "really was."

This reconstruction, it is supposed, will be more "true" because it corresponds more closely with the "facts" (since there is no interpretive framework) and because it is internally coherent (since it has been purged of discrepant elements). When Jesus is rendered "consistently" as a sage without admixture of apocalypticism, for example, that is thought "truer" to what Jesus really considered himself to be.

The attempt to get at a Jesus "behind" the Gospels (a Jesus unaffected by the perspective of belief) is stymied by the fact that—apart from a few scraps of evidence from pagan and Jewish sources sufficient to support the merest facts about him—absolutely everything we know about Jesus comes from communities of belief. It is not simply that the Gospels shape the memories in accordance with certain convictions; it is that the memories themselves were selected and shaped by people with the same convictions. We possess no "neutral" evidence concerning Jesus that can be appropriated for an alternative profile.

The effort also reveals a simplistic understanding of personal identity. There is something naive in the assumption that Jesus' own conception of himself—even if that were to be available—would be a truer indicator of his identity than the perceptions of his followers. One of the most important indicators of personal identity is the impact one has on others. The measurement of such impact is by definition inaccessible to oneself. But it is nevertheless an essential element in personal identity.

We would scarcely accept the self-understanding of Adolf Hitler— even if it were accompanied by a complete file of his sayings!—as an adequate representation of his identity. We cannot exclude the effect of his charismatic personality and destructive urges on others from the profile of his identity. If it were simply a matter of what he said and thought, he could just as well have been a mad painter in a Viennese attic as a demented despot. The evidence of how others *heard* what he said and *acted* on what he said is as critical to understanding his identity as his own writing and speech.

A more benign example is Mother Teresa. She seems to have been utterly consistent in thinking and declaring herself "only" a simple sister in service to the poor; neither her speech nor her attitude betrayed that self-understanding. Yet Mother Teresa's identity cannot be disconnected from her religious and social impact. The veneration of her as a saint that began in the last years of her life and the questioning of her political behavior that started immediately after her death are both significant dimensions of who she "really was." For personalities such as Hitler, Mother Teresa, and John F. Kennedy, the "historical truth" is always plural and complex precisely because these individuals are of historic significance, and what others have to say about them—admirers and detractors alike—is as pertinent as what they have to say for and about themselves.

Despite the impact that all of these figures had on the world, none of them was, like Jesus, a teacher and healer executed as a criminal under Roman authority and then—if his followers through the centuries are to be believed—raised from the dead and made powerfully alive with God's own life! How could the apprehension of any such figure ever be simple and straightforward?

Contemporary questers after the historical Jesus behind the Gospels complain that because those narratives are composed from the perspective of faith, they distort the "real Jesus." As the questers see it, they have been trying to recover some usable scraps from a decidedly unsatisfactory framework. Only slowly are they realizing that their pile of pieces does not amount to anything. A stack of film clips does not make a movie. A collection of anecdotes does not make a novel. A set of sayings and incidents about Jesus does not amount to a person. Why? Because personal identity is not about facts but about character. The question "Who are you?" is not answered satisfactorily by a driver's license listing one's vital statistics or by a curriculum vitae listing one's positions and accomplishments, for "Who are you?" is a question not so much about the *facts* of existence as about the *manner* of existence: "Based on how you have lived your life, what kind of person are you?" And this question is best answered by the story of one's life—often as narrated by others!

In place of the Gospel accounts of Jesus, then, the questers supply a quasi-narrative framework. The "authentic" Jesus materials are fitted into some ancient social category: Jesus the Sage, Jesus the Charismatic, Jesus the Revolutionary, Jesus the Peasant. Knowledge about such ancient social types is then used to fill out and frame the salvageable bits of Gospel material in order to provide a more complete profile of Jesus than the small collection of pieces enables.

The result, called the historical Jesus, is allowed precisely the range of possibilities envisaged for the ancient social category selected: if most peasants could not read, neither could Jesus; if some sages lacked eschatology, so did Jesus. Jesus must be one-dimensional and consistent precisely in the fashion that sociological categories must be one-dimensional and consistent. But this is not real history. It is a form of sociological typecasting.

History is about the ways in which people of the past managed to *transcend* their social settings. Socrates was not every Athenian citizen, Caesar was not every Roman aristocrat, Marcus Aurelius was not every Roman emperor, Epictetus and Spartacus were not every slave, and Jesus was not every Palestinian Jewish peasant! The reason that the questers' renderings of Jesus end up being so banal is that they are actually abstractions. Because they demand of their "Jesus image" perfect clarity and consistency, that image lacks the specificity and complexity that are the marks of real human existence. As a result, in their effort to make Jesus more "human" they have in fact made him more abstract than any creed could manage.

The Embrace of Multiplicity

The church rejected the "solutions" to multiplicity offered respectively by Marcion and Tatian. It canonized the four narrative Gospels in all their diversity. In so doing, the church implicitly affirmed the value of the Gospels as witnesses to and interpretations of the person of Jesus rather than as factually accurate biographies. It asserted that the ways in which these diverse narratives speak the truth about Jesus' character are more important than the ways in which they err concerning his exact words or deeds. In effect, the church stated—and continues to state—that in the case of the person of Jesus, truth is *not* single but plural. Rather than being captured by a single voice, Jesus is witnessed to by four reliable voices.

While we were still naive about the constructive character of photography, it was customary to draw the distinction between a portrait and a photograph of a person. Now we know that not even photographs are neutral representations of reality; on the contrary, they are profoundly perspectival and interpretive—even when not worked and reworked in the darkroom! The inclusion of subjects, the angle of vision, the moment of snapping the shutter, the decision about how to crop—in all these ways the photographer contributes even to the simplest of pictures. Still, the photographer is relatively passive once these decisions are made, dependent on what the subject does and how the light falls.

A painter obviously has much more interpretive control than a photographer does. Indeed, this continues to be the appeal of portraiture. We recognize in a fine portrait the way in which the subject and the painter have engaged in a long process of intersubjective learning, and if the painter is a good learner as well as a skilled artisan, the "truth" about the subject is revealed all the more profoundly because of the personal involvement and perspective of the portraitist. A caricature is a quick sketch that captures some salient physical mark and exaggerates it in such fashion as to evoke something of the person. And even that hasty process can produce remarkable art. But portraiture takes time, and what it reveals has less to do with physical appearance than it does with the state of the subject's soul. What distinguishes great portraiture is not the capacity to represent external reality so much as the ability to reveal internal reality. "It looks just like her" is not the best response to portraiture; rather, "That's *her*." The degree to which another can see the character of the subject in the portrait is the degree to which we consider the portrait *true*.

If we should have four great portraits of any single subject, we would consider ourselves indeed fortunate, precisely because of the ways in which the learning process carried on between subject and portraitist yields subtly (or perhaps even startlingly) different aspects of the same subject. How fascinating it is when we are able to "see" and "recognize" the same subject in several portraits even when the depictions are, in detail after detail, so different as to be untransferable from one painting to another.

The analogy between Gospel and portrait is, of course, only an analogy. In the first place, a literary narrative is a far more resistant medium than paint, and it can lead to far more "readings" than a portrait. In the second place, the evangelists were not "eyewitnesses" who walked about with Jesus and observed him over a period of time and then sought to depict him in story. The evangelists were Christians who constructed their narratives out of memories about Jesus passed on through the process of oral tradition in the churches over a period of some thirty to forty years after the death of Jesus. Certainly some of these memories *are* originally from eyewitnesses and first hearers. But even those memories underwent a process of selecting and shaping as they were handed on. The selection and shaping of memories was not arbitrary; it took place in response to the continuing experience of the risen Jesus in the church and to the multiple ways in which "learning Jesus" continued in communities after his death and resurrection.

Although they were not themselves eyewitnesses, then, the evangelists were certainly not "making Jesus up" in accordance with their own fantasies or "marketing the Messiah" (as one recent book put it) in order to adapt him to cultural standards. They were constrained in multiple ways: by their communities' ongoing experience of the resurrected Jesus in multiple embodiments (especially the ritual meal), by the facts about Jesus' life that were circulating from the beginning in the churches, by the ways in which the significance of Jesus' life and death and resurrection was being read in light of Torah, and above all by the understanding of his human character as obedient to God and loving toward other people.

In this respect, the analogy with portraiture is helpful: just as the portraitist needs to sit with the subject over time, observing and learning from such intersubjective exchange, so do the evangelists profit from the long period during which the memory of Jesus was handed on in communities of worship. The cost of such intersubjective learning may be a lack of distance, of objectivity, and certainly of accuracy in detail. But the gain is even greater, for the character of the subject is confirmed both by the memory of the past and by the continuing experience of him in the present.

We see, then, that the Gospels are not simple reportage. Neither are they caricatures dashed off with a bit of charcoal in a few moments. They are portraits thick with a texture resulting from long reflection, frequent repainting, and (in the case of two of them) the use of an earlier rendition.

The three Synoptic Gospels are not independent but interrelated witnesses to Jesus. All critical scholars agree that one of them was written first, and most conclude that it was Mark's Gospel. Matthew and Luke then each used Mark's version in composing both their own Gospels. They not only edited Mark, however; they also added other memories of Jesus. Some of these additional materials look so much alike that scholars have concluded that they may have been drawn from one or another written source available to both evangelists (a source conventionally called Q, for the German word *Quelle*, or "source"). Other materials look so different that they are usually thought to have come from Matthew's and Luke's respective special sources. Even the Gospel of John, which in the view of most scholars did not make use of the Synoptic Gospels in their finished form, used many of the same traditions as those employed by the Synoptics.

Despite these literary interrelationships, each of the Gospels presents Jesus in a distinctive way. The church embraces the Gospels in their multiplicity as pointers to a reality still richer and more complex than they can comprehend. As we approach each of them in turn—and I encourage you to approach the primary source before tackling my commentary in each case—we ask the same questions we asked of the other New Testament compositions. What sort of literary characteristics ought to be noted? How is the present and future reality of Jesus understood? What can we learn about the humanity of Jesus, particularly his character? And finally, how does the narrative understand the process of being a disciple—that is, a "learner" of Jesus?

CHAPTER 8

Jesus in Mark's Gospel

Before discussing Mark's narrative, we would do well to pause and consider the difference between the sort of reading that is truly appropriate to one seeking in the Holy Spirit to "learn Jesus" and the quasi-didactic analysis that is the best one can do when writing a book. Writing a book about reading Mark is not the same as reading Mark. Even more so, reading a book written about reading Mark is no replacement for reading Mark!

The reading of Mark that gives life and enables the learning of Jesus is the slow, deliberate, ruminative, associative reading of his story in sequence—a kind of reading that is simply impossible to replace by any mode of analysis. The reading I mean is really an aspect of that "intersubjective learning" I described in Chapter 4. It involves entrusting one's spirit to the Spirit, which can work through the act of reading; it takes time and patience and repetition and silence and creative fidelity. And it involves suffering.

Such reading of the sacred page was the main mechanism of the spiritual life in antiquity and through much of the Middle Ages. The point was not to find an answer but to linger in a question, not to solve a riddle but to live with a mystery. "Spiritual reading" in this classical mode is still the most valuable way to engage any of the Gospels. For that matter, it is the best way to read *any* of the New Testament writings, if we hope from such reading to make possible a transformation of our minds in the image of Christ. With narrative texts, however, such a patient following along with the story is demanded by the shape of the compositions themselves. The best that my remarks can do is to point to some of the ways in which such reading might usefully be informed.

Approaching Mark's Gospel

It is important to remember that although Mark's is the first narrative Gospel known to us—and may well have been the first to be composed—his was not the first telling of the story of Jesus. We have seen in the letters of Paul and other first-generation writers a remarkable range of information concerning the humanity of Jesus, and—above all in Paul—an implied story that could be used by way of allusion and application. Paul did not have to tell the story about Jesus to his readers, for they already knew it, even in churches that had not been founded by Paul (the church at Rome, for example). We are most certain that some account of Jesus' passion circulated early—in sketchy form perhaps already in the first days of the movement, but progressively gaining more richness as the full implications of reading Jesus' death through the words of the prophets were realized. Thus Paul can chide the Galatians "before whose eyes Christ was displayed as crucified" (Gal. 3:1), and for the Romans can apply to the suffering of Jesus verses of the same Psalm 68 that was also used in shaping the passion accounts (Rom. 15:3).

That this loose framework was in place shortly after Jesus' death tells us that the evangelist composed his account against the backdrop of an implied story about Jesus, and that his readers read his version against the backdrop of the story already in their possession. The best evidence for this within Mark's narrative itself is the way in which he introduces characters and places without any explanation. This practice makes sense only if we assume that readers already know such information. In his opening lines (1:1–9), for example, Mark speaks of John and Jordan and Isaiah and Jesus and Galilee, without any introductory or explanatory remarks enabling his readers to place those figures and places. Present-day readers are not jolted by the technique precisely because—like Mark's first readers—they have other stories with which to fill the gaps in Mark. Where they do not have such information—as when Mark in 3:6 mentions the

Herodians (about whom we otherwise know nothing) or in 15:21 alludes to the relatives of Simon of Cyrene as though they should be recognized—present-day readers appreciate how allusive and dependent on a larger story Mark's narrative really is.

At the same time, we should not think that the larger narrative context necessarily included the specific materials with which Mark worked, or ordered them in the same way. Mark's narrative is Mark's construction. It is true that with information gleaned from the epistolary literature, we are able to recognize in Mark a rough shared framework: Jesus was born of a woman (6:3) under the law (1:44) and was descended from David (10:47; 11:10). He prayed to God as "Abba" (14:36). He was tested (1:13), shared a last Passover meal with his disciples (14:12–25), was arrested (14:46) with the assistance of Jewish leaders, underwent a trial before Pontius Pilate (15:1–15), was crucified (15:21), and was buried (15:46).

But Mark fills this framework with a number of incidents about which there is no mention in the letters: the baptism of John and Jesus' participation in it (1:4–11), the death of the Baptist (6:14–29), Jesus' selection of certain people as disciples (1:16–20; 2:14), all the stories of his healing and exorcising (e.g., 1:21–31, 40–45), all the words of teaching (e.g., 4:1–33; 13:5–37), his journeys (e.g., 4:35; 6:1, 45, 53; 8:27; 10:1), his feeding of the crowds (6:30–44; 8:1–10), his entry into Jerusalem (11:1–10), his cleansing of the temple (11:11–19), his confrontations with Jewish leaders (12:1–40).

All of these materials, furthermore, are organized by Mark according to his own compositional principles. If we read only the Synoptic Gospels, it is easy to forget this important point because they make such heavy use of the Markan sequence, but when we compare Mark to John, we perceive that the Synoptic order of events is not a simple report of events as they happened. Only a little thought is necessary to recognize how unlikely it is that Jesus told all his parables in one sitting, or had all his controversies with Jewish opponents at the beginning and end of his ministry, or experienced testing on only two occasions, or spoke of the end-time in only one discourse. Between the baptism of John and the burial of Jesus—with the probable exception of the main events of the passion—the ordering of the materials in Mark's Gospel is in all likelihood a result of Mark's rhetorical strategies.

Let me offer three final observations by way of introducing Mark's narrative. The first is that Mark's approach to the material—his narrative format and sequencing—was his own choice. Although, as we have seen, there is good evidence for a broad "story of Jesus" in circulation before Mark, there is no real evidence that any of the discrete memories of Jesus' sayings and deeds—except, once more, the passion account—had been placed into a narrative framework. As far as we can tell, Mark was the first to do it.

The second observation is that, faced with this task, Mark could have constructed the story of Jesus in any number of ways. He could, for example, have used only miracle stories and presented Jesus as a wonder-worker. Conversely, he could have used only Jesus' sayings and presented him as a sage. But Mark chose to use both kinds of stories from the oral tradition, so that both Jesus' powerful deeds and his wisdom became part of his portrait. But Mark's most decisive choice was to not only connect all of these memories to a disproportionately lengthy and detailed passion account, but also to construct his narrative so that everything before the passion and death of Jesus also pointed toward it. In other words, Mark chose to tell his explicit story about Jesus within that framework that we have already seen in the epistolary literature to be normative for Christian identity.

The third observation is that Mark's way of telling the story focuses exclusively on the identity of Jesus and the drama of discipleship: who Jesus is and what it means to be his "learner" (mathētēs). Matthew and Luke open their accounts to larger concerns, situating the story of Jesus respectively in the contexts of formative Judaism and the Gentile mission, while John elevates the drama to the level of cosmic significance. But Mark

stays tightly focused on Jesus and his followers. This does not make him
the most important of our witnesses, but it certainly makes him one of un-
usual power.

The Complexity of Mark's Image of Jesus

Although the first quest for the historical Jesus described by Albert
Schweitzer in 1906 hoped that the determination of the earliest Gospel
would result in the discovery of a "simple" Jesus, Mark decisively disap-
points that expectation. His thickly textured portrait reveals not only Jesus
"as he was" but above all Jesus "as he is now perceived" by the eyes of
faith.

The faith perspective is obvious from the first words: "The beginning
of the good news about Jesus Christ, Son of God" (Mark 1:1). Readers
know from the start that this is not simply a story about a woodworker
from Nazareth; it is a proclamation of Jesus as "Messiah," one whose identity is defined by a specific role in history and by the symbols of a specific
people. His story, furthermore, is an *archē* ("beginning"), serving as both
the chronological starting point and the enduring foundation for the *euangelion* ("good news"). Mark's use of the term *good news* within his narrative makes it clear that he is reading Jesus' past through the lens of the
experience of a community that continues to live in Jesus' name. Jesus
preaches the "good news" and calls people to "believe in the good news"
(1:14–15). He declares that those who leave their possessions and relationships "for my sake and for the sake of the good news" will receive a reward
in this life "and in the age to come eternal life" (10:29). He declares that before the coming of the Son of man, the "good news must be preached to all
the nations" (13:10) and says of the woman who anointed him for his burial
that "wherever the good news is preached" she would be remembered
(14:9). Mark's use of this *euangelion* terminology makes his faith perspective on the story of Jesus transparent.

Mark's first line also tells us that this good news concerns Jesus as

"Son of God" (1:1). Paul speaks of Jesus "designated as Son of God in power" through the resurrection (Rom. 1:3), but Mark reads the entire human ministry of Jesus through that lens, even though up to the point of his death no humans had recognized Jesus as God's Son. It is God's voice from heaven in the baptism that calls him "my Son" (1:11), and God's voice from the cloud at the transfiguration that proclaims, "This is my Son" (9:7). The demonic forces that enslave humans also recognize that Jesus is "the Holy One of God" (1:24) and "God's Son" (3:11; 5:7), who has come to do away with their power. The reader is to understand the baptism and the transfiguration as moments of revelation in which Jesus' full identity is made known.

From the beginning of Mark's narrative, therefore, the reader is invited to share the perception of Jesus as God's Child and the Holy One of God. What the author and readers—and within the narrative, both God and demons—know from the beginning, however, the human characters in the narrative do not realize. The tension between these perspectives makes Mark's narrative intensely ironic.

Mark's understanding of Jesus as Son of God certainly owes something to his postresurrection perspective. Some readers have concluded from Mark's failure to relate any explicit appearance accounts that he did not consider Jesus to be the resurrected one. The fallacy of reaching conclusions from silence has never been more obvious. Mark does not relate appearance accounts, it is true, and no doubt has his reasons for that choice. But can any careful reader really think that Mark did not consider Jesus to have been raised and to have appeared to his followers? In each of his three passion predictions, as reported in Mark, Jesus concludes with the explicit statement that the Son of man "will be raised up after three days" (8:31; 9:32; 10:34). In response to John and James's request for a place on his right hand or his left "when he entered into his glory" (10:37), Jesus does not deny that he will enter into glory, only that it is not his to bestow positions at the right hand or the left (10:40). At the last meal, Jesus tells his disciples, "After I am raised up, I will go before you to Galilee" (14:27), and the messenger at the tomb tells the women, "He Is going before you to Galilee. You will see him there" (16:7). Finally, after the transfiguration, Jesus instructs his disciples to tell no one about what they had experienced, "until the Son of man is raised from the dead" (9:9). Is it conceivable that Mark—who had control over these very materials—should have created such anticipation, generated precisely by the most reliable voice in the narrative, and then want the reader to conclude that it did not happen? The exact opposite is, I think, the case: it is because it was so well known to Mark's readers that Jesus *did* rise and appear to followers after his glorification that Mark is able to make a literary and religious point by withholding descriptions of explicit appearances. In my judgment, Mark wants his readers to understand Jesus' resurrection not simply as an event of the past but also and precisely as a dimension of the present: Jesus can still be encountered by Gospel readers.

In his narrative, Mark clearly hints at Jesus' continuing presence in the church. I have noted, for example, that he has Jesus pronounce a promise of eternal life for those who leave all "for my sake and the sake of the good news" (10:29). Jesus also predicts that in the future his disciples will "suffer for my sake" (13:9), and that when persecuted they will be supported by the Holy Spirit (13:11). Conversely, everyone who receives Jesus' disciples is also receiving him, and the one receiving him receives the one who sent him (9:37); likewise, the one who gives a disciple a cup of water because he "bear[s] the name of Christ" will be rewarded (9:41).

In Mark's Gospel the coming of the Son of man in the future is not the replacement for resurrection faith (as has sometimes been suggested) but rather its logical extension. This is at least one reason why Jesus is associated with Moses and Elijah in the transfiguration account (9:4). The scene follows directly upon Jesus' self-referential statement in 8:38 to the effect that the Son of man would come in glory, and that "some of those standing here" would not die before seeing "the kingdom of God come in glory"

(9:1). Within the Jewish tradition, Moses and Elijah were figures who had ascended to God's presence and were consequently expected to return in the future. The disciples' glimpse of Jesus with Moses and Elijah on the mountain is surely meant to convey that Jesus also is a figure who goes to God's presence and will return, although in unique fashion: "This is my Son, the beloved: listen to him" (9:7).

In his eschatological discourse also Jesus declares that the Son of man will come "on the clouds with great power and glory" (13:26), and in response to the high priest's question whether he is the Christ, the Son of the Blessed One, Jesus answers, "I am. And you will see the Son of man, sitting at the right hand of the Power and coming with the clouds of heaven" (14:62).

Even during his human life, moreover, Mark's Jesus reveals a depth of being and of power that points to an origin in God. His first words—"The time has come to completion, and the rule of God has come; turn about and believe the good news" (1:15)—are at the very least those of a human person who claims to know the course of history and God's plan and has the prophetic authority to call people to change their lives. When he is asked by the demons why he has "come" (1:23), and when he himself declares "why I came" (1:38), he asserts, "I have come not to call the righteous but sinners" (2:17); such language points to an extraordinary sense of mission. Similarly, Jesus declares, self-referentially, that "the Son of man has power on earth to forgive sins" (2:10) and that "the Son of man is Lord of the Sabbath" (2:28). Not only is Jesus called "Son" by God (1:11; 9:7), but he calls God "Papa" *(Abba)* in return (14:36). Although Jesus eschews knowledge of the end-time, in so doing he refers to God as his Father and to himself as Son (13:32), and does so immediately after declaring that "heaven and earth will pass away but my words will not pass away" (13:31).

It is not simply that Jesus' speech and the declaration of God reveal his special status, however. Mark shows Jesus working wonders—feeding the multitudes (6:30–44; 8:1–10), stilling the storm (4:35–40), walking on the water (6:45–52)—that demonstrate a power over creation itself and demand an answer to the question "Who therefore is this person that even the wind and the sea obey him?" (4:41).

In addition to emphasizing Jesus' divinity, Mark also makes a distinctive contribution to the rendering of Jesus' humanity, first by portraying him in the social role of teacher. Jesus' townspeople think of him as a *tektōn*, a worker in wood, and they recognize him only as the son of Mary and as the brother of James and Joses and Jude and Simon (6:3). Mark himself portrays Jesus as a *didaskalos*, however—one whose activities correspond to those of Greco-Roman philosophers: Jesus gathers disciples to travel with him and share his life, he teaches in public places and in private, and he gives special instruction to his students. Indeed, Mark uses the title "teacher"—*didaskalos* or *rabbi*—of Jesus proportionately more frequently than either Luke or Matthew (see 4:38; 5:35; 9:5, 17, 38; 10:17, 20, 35, 51; 11:21; 12:14, 19, 32; 13:1; 14:14, 45). It is a title, furthermore, by which Jesus is known to all other categories of human characters in the narrative—not only his disciples but also those seeking his help and those who oppose him.

Despite the characterization of Jesus as teacher, however, Mark includes in his narrative relatively little of Jesus' speech: a proclamation of the kingdom, a series of pronouncements, and a handful of parables, calls, warnings, and predictions. And Jesus' teaching, as exhibited in Mark, is no more illuminating than it is extensive. His words appear as both demanding and deflective; they contain at least as much obscurity as clarity. Indeed, Mark seems to make Jesus himself the main thing to be taught. His is the presence that needs to be grasped; he is the parable that embodies the "mystery of the kingdom" (4:11).

Jesus is indeed "mystery" in Mark's Gospel, a figure so complex as to resist understanding even when revealed. At least in part this is due to the intrinsic difficulty of combining in one figure the power of God at work in the world and a fragile and suffering humanity. It is not surprising, then,

that throughout the narrative Jesus eludes human grasp. Though designated "Son of God" by the voice from heaven and the cries of demons, the
only human character to declare him "God's Son" is the centurion at the
cross (15:39). It is not at the moment of overt victory over evil that Jesus is
declared God's Son, but at the moment when evil appears triumphant—
and then by the agent of execution! We cannot look to Mark for a Jesus who
is simple and uncomplicated, someone "just like us."

We can move more deeply into Mark's complex portrayal of Jesus' humanity by examining his use of the designation "Son of man." The title appears only in the Gospel materials—apart from a single appearance in
Revelation 1:13—and is always associated with Jesus. It may well derive
from Jesus' own usage, since it makes sense as a self-reference in Aramaic
in a way that it does not in Greek. In any case, Mark's Gospel is our earliest
datable example of the application of that designation to Jesus, and in that
narrative it is always Jesus who uses it of himself. Some people think that
we find Jesus' own self-understanding in the sayings where the designation appears. I think it more accurate to say that we get Mark's portrayal of
Jesus' self-understanding, but that is still remarkably valuable testimony.

I have already noted two of the ways in which Jesus uses the title "Son
of man" with reference to himself. The first is in connection with his present authority as a teacher: he is Lord of the Sabbath (2:28) and has authority to forgive sins (2:10). The second is in connection with his exaltation
and future coming: he will be raised from the dead (9:9) and come on the
clouds in glory (8:38; 13:26; 14:62). If these were the only ways Mark used
the title, it would point only to Jesus' power and glory.

Mark's most distinctive way of using Son of man language, however,
is in connection with Jesus' suffering. In each of his passion predictions,
Jesus speaks of the Son of man having to undergo rejection and suffering
(8:31; 9:31; 10:33). After the transfiguration, Jesus states (in 9:12) that it is
part of the divine plan that "the Son of man should suffer many things,"
and at the Last Supper he declares, "For the Son of man goes as it is written

of him. But woe to that one by whom the Son of man is handed over" (14:21). In other words, Jesus himself supplies the interpretation of his death: he accepts the death that comes to him as a result of human betrayal because that is what God wills and what is written of the Messiah in Scripture. Mark puts a dramatic human face on this proposition when he pictures Jesus before his arrest in the most profound emotional anguish, praying, "Abba, Father, all things are possible to you. Let this cup pass from me. Yet not as I will but as you will" (14:36). Jesus' obedience to the Father is not easy, for what is true of his followers who sleep is also true of him: the spirit is willing but the flesh is weak (14:38). He wants to live, asks to be allowed to live. Yet he allows the "project" to which God calls him to relativize his own aspirations.

The final Son of man saying that we consider leads us to the other dimension of Mark's understanding of Jesus' suffering. It is not only an expression of faithful obedience to God; it is also an act of faithful service to other people. Jesus declares to his disciples, "For the Son of man did not come to be served but to serve, and to give his life as a ransom for many" (10:45). Mark expresses the self-giving character of Jesus' death in his description of Jesus' last meal with his disciples. Jesus breaks the bread and gives it to them, declaring, "This is my body, given for you." And he shares the cup, telling them, "This is the blood of the covenant poured out for many" (14:22–25).

Mark not only has Jesus state this pattern; he also shows it narratively. If we follow the narrative sequence that begins in 1:21, we see that Jesus' proclamation of the kingdom and his teaching in the synagogue are interrupted by the need to exorcise a demon (1:21–27). At the home of Peter, Jesus is called on to heal Peter's mother-in-law (1:29–31). This healing draws the attention of the whole town as crowds surround the house where he is staying. He cannot return to teaching but must continue to heal (1:32–34). When he gets up early to be by himself, he is sought out by Peter, who reminds him of still more people desiring his healing touch. But

Jesus refuses, clinging to his original project, his own understanding of what God has called him to do. He decides to go on to other towns, preaching rather than healing, "for that is what I came out to do" (1:35–39). Jesus wants to *preach*. But in the very next passage, we find Jesus accosted by a man who has leprosy and seeks healing from him (1:41–45). Jesus is "moved with compassion" and accedes to the man's desire: "I will it; be made clean." We could certainly understand if one of the intriguing textual variants were original: instead of *splangknistheis* ("moved with compassion"), it reads *orgistheis* ("moved with anger"). Jesus is certainly serving rather than being served in this series of incidents, and that service comes at considerable cost. Note also the end of this story: Jesus and the man with leprosy exchange places. The man who had been in the wilderness is restored to society and does Jesus' job of preaching! But Jesus' notoriety is so great that he seeks even greater solitude in the desert—yet *still* the crowds come to him, undoubtedly to be served (1:45).

A similar narrative sequence occurs in Mark 6:7–44. Jesus cannot meet all the needs of the people himself, so he gives his followers a share in his ministry: they too are to preach the kingdom and drive out demons (6:7–13). When they return from their mission, they join efforts with Jesus, but the press of the crowd seeking healing is so great that Jesus and the disciples have no time even to eat. He therefore tells them to come away with him to a desert place (6:30–32). Again, Jesus seeks a legitimate project of his own: to be "served" by company of his own in a restful place. But the crowd sees him leaving and goes on ahead of him across the water (6:33). When Jesus arrives at the far shore, he looks up and sees the crowd approaching. Once more, Mark notes that he is "filled with compassion," for the crowd is like "sheep without a shepherd" (6:34). Jesus again relativizes his own project and enters into the service of the people. In that desert place, he "teaches them many things" (6:34), and then, when it grows too late for them to return, he feeds them—all five thousand—on the side of the mountain (6:35–44). It is no accident that Mark has Jesus "bless and break" this bread that he distributes to the crowd, for the feeding points forward to his last meal with the disciples, when he "blesses and breaks and gives" to them. Each of these meals in turn points to the ultimate body language of the cross, where in obedience to God, Jesus "gives his life as a ransom for many," just as he did all during his ministry.

Following Jesus

It is natural for us, as it was for Mark's first readers, to identify with those characters in his narrative who are called "disciples" or "learners" *(mathē-tai)*, since their relationship to Jesus during his ministry can be taken as at least structurally analogous to our relationship to Jesus as the Resurrected One. It would also be natural for us to look to the disciples as models for our own learning of Jesus: we should learn Jesus in the way they did. But Mark's narrative confounds this expectation.

One side of Mark's portrayal of the disciples emphasizes their special position. They are selected by Jesus from among the crowd to be "with him" and share his work (3:14). It is to them that the "mystery of the kingdom of God" has been given (4:11). Jesus reveals to them his identity as suffering Son of man (8:31), and they have a glimpse of his status as glorious Son of God (9:2–8). They hear his secret discourse about the tribulations to come and the triumphant coming of the Son of man (13:5–37). The other side of Mark's portrayal stresses the disciples' inadequacy. Although as "insiders" they are expected to understand the things taught by their teacher, they show themselves to be remarkably inept learners. They do not understand the parables (4:13) or Jesus' actions (4:31; 6:52)—or even his plain speech (7:17). Above all, they fail to understand his clear predictions of his death and resurrection (8:21).

Worse than their ignorance, however, is their infidelity. Their lack of understanding is comprehensible, given the shocking character of Jesus' self-revelation. But they also fail to stay "with him" as he moves toward his suffering and death. One disciple betrays Jesus for money (14:10–11). One denies even knowing him (14:66–72). And when Jesus is arrested, they "all flee" (14:50). Only at the very end, in the angel's message to the women at the tomb, does Mark hold out hope for these stupid and faithless followers. If they go to Galilee, if they "follow Jesus" there, then they will see him (16:7); the Resurrected One offers hope even to those who miserably fail him during his life.

What narrative purpose does Mark have in shaping this portrait? It seems less likely that he was using the disciples in an attempt to discredit despised leaders in his church than that he was deliberately using the disciples as a foil for the figure of Jesus and as a means of warning his readers against imitating them rather than Jesus. We can see this most clearly in the way Mark has arranged his materials following Peter's recognition of Jesus as the Messiah in 8:29. Jesus proceeds to teach them "plainly" that the Son of man must suffer and die before being raised (8:31). Peter rebukes Jesus for this teaching (8:32) and is in turn rebuked for "being not on the side of God but of humans" (8:33). This is followed by Jesus' teaching on discipleship: being a disciple means self-denial, taking up the cross and following Jesus, and losing one's life for his sake and the sake of the good news (8:34–37).

The second passion prediction in 9:31 is likewise followed by the disciples' incomprehension (9:32), as demonstrated by their subsequent discussion concerning who among them is the greatest (9:33–34). Jesus teaches them first by declaring that greatness is a matter of service: "If anyone would be first, that one must be the last of all and the servant of all" (9:35). Then Jesus places a child in their midst and says, "Whoever receives one among such children in my name receives me, and whoever receives me receives not me but the one who sent me" (9:37). The third passion prediction in 10:32–34 is once more followed by a misunderstanding of discipleship. John and James want to claim places on Jesus' right hand and left when he comes in his glory (9:38). Jesus uses the opportunity to combine the two lessons made previously, connecting discipleship directly to the character of his role as Messiah:

> You know that those who are supposed to rule over the Gentiles lord it over them, and their great men exercise authority over them. But it shall not be so among you; but whoever would be great among you must be your servant, and whoever would be first among you must be slave of all. For the Son of man also came not to be served but to serve and to give his life as a ransom for many. (10:42–45, RSV)

The disciples in Mark's narrative consistently misunderstand the nature of Jesus' role as suffering servant who gives his life for others. They think only of his coming glory and their share in it. They therefore also fail to understand that to "follow" Jesus means to "be with him" through such suffering. And because they do not grasp this, they also fail to remain loyal to Jesus through his suffering.

Mark wants readers not to imitate the disciples but to follow Jesus. Thus he introduces the last of these two moments of misunderstanding and correction with the transfiguration, an event that concludes with a voice from the cloud identifying Jesus as the beloved Son and saying, "Listen to him" (9:7). The message is meant not for the men on the mountain but for readers of the narrative: as they follow Jesus through the text on his way to Jerusalem, they should attend not to what the disciples are saying but to what Jesus is saying and doing, and learn from him what it means to be God's servant in the world.

Mark joins in the closest possible fashion his understanding of Jesus and his understanding of discipleship. To "learn Jesus" in this Gospel is not to confuse the present power of the resurrected Jesus with a realized kingdom in which one deserves a place of authority and privilege. It is instead to learn how to be little and weak, a servant who in the pattern of Jesus gives one's life as a ransom for others.

CHAPTER 9

Jesus in Matthew's Gospel

Matthew the evangelist (whoever he may have been) both approved the Gospel of Mark and sought to improve it. His approval is shown by his appropriation of most of Mark's composition into his own. Matthew follows Mark's story line from the baptism of John to the empty tomb, editing this Markan narrative spine fairly vigorously. By moving things around a bit and considerably reducing Mark's verbosity, he tells the Markan story with greater economy. Matthew does not, however, alter either the basic lines of Mark's story or Mark's understanding of Jesus and discipleship. If anything, he strengthens each of the elements in Mark's complex portrayal.

Matthew alters Mark most by adding new material concerning Jesus. The major narrative additions are the account of Jesus' birth (chaps. 1–2) and two resurrection appearance stories (28:8–20). These serve to connect Jesus respectively to the story of Israel and the life of the church. More impressive is the substantial discourse material that Matthew injects into the Markan story line. Some of the included sayings of Jesus are found also in Luke and may well have come from the hypothesized written source (or sources) that scholars designate as Q. Other sayings are distinctive to Matthew. Matthew arranges all these sayings into discrete discourses (chaps. 5–7, 10, 13, 18, 23–25).

The effect of adding so much discourse material is to heighten the portrayal of Jesus as a teacher in word as well as in action. Since many of these sayings serve both to locate Jesus within Judaism and to instruct members of the church—Matthew uses the term *ekklēsia* ("church") explicitly in 16:18 and 18:17—it is clear that this Gospel takes Mark's tight drama of discipleship and opens it to the broader social concerns facing Matthew's readers. Learning Jesus in this Gospel definitely involves learning from the words of Jesus the teacher. This is so much the case that readers of Matthew have sometimes tended to pay attention *only* to the words of Jesus (for example, in the Sermon on the Mount in chaps. 5–7), neglecting the important ways in which Matthew has Jesus teach by the character of his life. Matthew closely links the instructions spoken by Jesus and the instructive character of the people in his narrative—above all, the character of Jesus himself.

Before turning to Matthew's distinctive shaping of Jesus' image, we can note ways that Matthew appropriates and extends elements of Mark's portrayal. The postresurrection perspective is certainly even more obvious in Matthew than it is in Mark. Matthew adds appearances of the risen Jesus to the women who went to the tomb (28:9–10) and to eleven of the disciples on a mountain in Galilee (28:16–20), thus giving the promise of 28:7—"He is going before you to Galilee; there you will see him" (compare Mark 16:7)—fulfillment within the narrative. The final appearance functions as a commissioning of the disciples. They are now to "go make disciples of all nations, baptizing them . . . teaching them to keep all the things that I have commanded you" (28:19).

The Gospel closes with Jesus' promise, "Behold, I am with you always, to the close of the age" (28:20), which indicates the continuing life and power of the risen Lord in the church. This declaration in turn echoes two earlier statements. Jesus says to his disciples in 18:20, "Where two or three are gathered in my name, there I am among them." The notion of Jesus being with them is given even deeper resonance by the angel's explanation of the name to be given Jesus: "His name will be called Emmanuel, which is translated as God with us" (1:23). Even more than Mark, then, Matthew shapes his story from the explicit standpoint of belief in Jesus as the Resurrected One who shares God's own life with the community to which he is present through time.

Matthew also extends Mark's emphasis on Jesus' humanity. The infancy account has the obvious effect of stressing Jesus' share in the human condition: his birth to a woman who has conceived by the Holy Spirit (1:20) continues a pattern of God's work among outcast women in Israel (1:3, 5, 6). Jesus' birth is overshadowed by the slaughter of the infants (2:16–27), which anticipates the violence that will befall the innocent Jesus as well. Matthew uses the designation "Son of man" even more frequently than Mark does; some of the sayings that use that designation—always in the mouth of Jesus and self-referential—point to the glorious future judgment (19:28; 24:27, 30, 36, 37, 39, 44; 25:31) or present authority (13:37; 18:11), but others stress the suffering of the Son of man (12:40; 26:2, 24, 45). Of particular importance (because it sets the framework for all the subsequent uses) is the first appearance of the title in Matthew's narrative: "Foxes have dens and birds of the air have nests, but the Son of man does not have a place to lay his head" (8:20). Finally, Matthew applies two particularly powerful citations from Torah to the work of Jesus. Commenting on Jesus' ministry of healing the sick, Matthew notes, "In order to fulfill what was spoken by the prophet Isaiah, 'He himself took our infirmities and bore our diseases'" (8:17; see Isa. 53:4). And when Jesus withdraws from a place because of a plot against him, Matthew further notes,

> This was to fulfill what was spoken by the prophet Isaiah: "Behold my servant whom I have chosen, my beloved with whom my soul is well pleased. I will put my spirit upon him, and he shall proclaim justice to the Gentiles. He will not wrangle or cry aloud, nor will anyone hear his voice in the streets; he will not break a bruised reed or quench a smoldering wick, till he brings justice to victory; and in his name will the Gentiles hope." (12:18–21, RSV)

These citations represent authorial commentary on the story of Jesus and show how thoroughly Jesus' ministry was interpreted in light of Torah. They also show how Matthew shares and even deepens Mark's understanding of Jesus' entire life as one defined by service to others.

Son of David, Son of God

We can approach Matthew's distinctive rendering of Jesus through his use of two titles. Each pertains to Jesus' human status and character, and each directs readers in ways they might not expect. The conviction that Jesus as Messiah was descended from David is attested in the epistolary literature (Rom. 1:3; 2 Tim. 2:8). In Mark's Gospel, too, Jesus is several times designated as "Son of David" (Mark 10:47–48; 11:10; 12:35). The title connects Jesus to traditional messianic expectations within Judaism. Matthew's extended use of it supports the suggestion that his Gospel was written in the context of a developing, formative Judaism. The Gospel's opening genealogy establishes the link emphatically by mentioning David repeatedly (1:1, 6, 17) and then stating explicitly that Joseph was a "son of David" (1:20). Matthew associates Jesus with the deeds of David (12:3) and has Jesus greeted as "Son of David" by the crowds (9:27; 15:22; 20:30–31; 21:9, 15). He thereby establishes a narrative foundation for the exchange between Jesus and the Pharisees in 22:41–46: building on their identification of the Messiah as "Son of David," Jesus asks how it is that David, in Psalm 110:1, calls him "Lord." For Matthew, Jesus truly is David's Son, but as the Resurrected One, he is more than simply a Jewish military leader; he is Lord. I will return later to the narrative importance of that distinction.

Another designation Matthew uses for Jesus is "Son of God." It would seem at first that this title simply indicates Jesus' divine status and logically contrasts with "Son of man" or "Son of David." Matthew's usage, however, is rooted in the traditions of Torah concerning Israel as God's Child. In 2:15 Matthew applies to Jesus the citation of Hosea 11:1: "Out of Egypt I have called my son" (see Exod. 4:22). By applying this passage to Jesus—a passage meant by the prophet as a reference to the people of Israel in the Exodus—Matthew identifies him as the faithful Child whom God had desired in Israel. Matthew's image of Jesus as Son of God is fundamentally relational: Jesus is the human person who is fully faithful and obedient to God's word. Jesus' testing in the wilderness—again, as for the people of old—demonstrates in what manner he is God's Son (4:1–11). Israel's hardships in the desert had led the people to "test the Lord" by complaint and rebellion (see Exod. 16:2; Num. 11:1; 14:1; Deut. 1:26; Ps. 95: 8–11; 106:13–25). The devil makes the issue explicit, saying to Jesus twice, "If you are God's Son . . ." (4:3, 6), holding out to Jesus the possibilities of pleasure, power, and divine protection. Jesus answers in the very words of Torah: "Humans shall not live by bread alone, but by every word that proceeds from the mouth of God" (4:4; see Deut. 8:3). Jesus is the obedient Child who perfectly fulfills the righteousness demanded by God in Torah (see 3:13–15) and is therefore able to proclaim that righteousness in his words to the people (5:1–7:28).

Matthew's crucifixion scene further demonstrates his understanding of Jesus as God's Son and offers a haunting reprise of the temptation account. The passion account in Matthew follows Mark's closely. One of his alterations is to have the Jewish populace as a whole claim responsibility for Jesus' death (27:25). Another is to have the entire populace pass by the cross and cry out derisively, "If you are Son of God, come down from the cross" (27:40; see 27:43). Their taunt is an echo of Satan's jeering challenge: "If you are Son of God, throw yourself down" (4:6). Surely a Son of God was one who could exercise such power and avoid a humiliating and painful death! But Jesus accepts his Father's will as he said he would (26:39) and is obedient to the end. When the centurion declares, "Truly this was God's Son" (27:54), Matthew's readers understand that such recognition was earned by Jesus' human fidelity and obedience to God.

Teacher and Lord

Jesus' most prominent activity in Matthew's Gospel is teaching. As Son, he knows the Father's will and can reveal it to others (11:25–30). Matthew's readers do not hear Jesus' words simply as the teachings of a dead sage, but as the commandments of a present and powerful Lord whose "words will never pass away" (24:35). Jesus is teacher precisely as the Lord of the church.

To make this point, Matthew edits Mark's narrative with extraordinary precision, drawing a distinction between the designation of Jesus as "teacher" (or "rabbi") and as "Lord." In Mark's Gospel, as I noted, everybody calls Jesus "teacher." On the other hand, only the afflicted in Mark call him "Lord" *(kyrios)*; his disciples never greet him with that term. Matthew has only outsiders call Jesus "teacher": opponents—such as the scribes (8:19; 12:38) and Pharisees (12:38; 22:16, 36), Jewish tax collectors (17:24), Herodians (22:16), and Sadducees (22:24)—and those who, like the rich man (19:16), encounter Jesus but do not come to belief. In contrast, Jesus is never called "teacher" by the disciples, the afflicted, or those coming to faith in him. The disciples call him "Lord" (*kyrios;* 8:25; 14:28; 16:22; 17:4; 18:21), as do those who are coming to belief in him (8:2, 6, 8; 9:27–31; 15:22, 25, 27; 20:30).

Matthew has a point to this careful editing of titles. For those Jews (and all others) who do not accept Jesus as risen Messiah, he is simply another teacher, like the rabbis of formative Judaism. For those who confess him as crucified and raised Messiah, while Jesus is a teacher (just as he is Son of David), he is also much more: he is the Lord who with "all authority" (28:18) teaches the church. The apparent exceptions prove the rule. In one case, Matthew has Jesus claim the title of teacher *for himself* in contrast to the "rabbis" among the scribes and Pharisees, but to do so he uses a term (*kathēgētēs* = "master," "instructor") otherwise unattested in the narrative (23:10). The second case concerns Judas, who betrays Jesus. The term *Lord* is never on his lips. When at the Last Supper Jesus predicts his betrayal, the other disciples ask, "Is it I, Lord?" (26:22). Judas, in contrast, asks, "Is it I, Rabbi?"(26:25). And when he arrives in the Garden of Gethsemane with those arresting Jesus, Judas greets Jesus with these words: "Hail, Rabbi" (26:49). Subtly but powerfully Matthew identifies Judas as an outsider.

Jesus and Torah

Matthew's Gospel was written in the context of conflict and conversation with the form of Judaism that developed out of the religious aspirations of the Pharisees and the textual interpretations of the scribes into what is known as *classical* or *rabbinic* Judaism after the destruction of the temple in 70 C.E. This can be seen above in the way Matthew's image of Jesus is shaped by appropriating the central symbol of that rival tradition—namely, Torah. One side of this shaping is found in the polemical attack on the scribes and Pharisees in Matthew 23, which functions within the story to castigate the teachers of the "synagogue down the street" and position Jesus as the messianic "instructor" of the church. The more positive side is found in the way Matthew uses the symbolism attached to Torah within the pharisaic tradition to communicate his understanding of Jesus.

Jesus appears most obviously as *teacher of Torah*. Having been delivered from Egypt and having passed through the waters of baptism and been tested in the wilderness, Jesus has shown himself to be the Righteous One who can interpret God's will. The Sermon on the Mount (chaps. 5–7) establishes Jesus as the messianic interpreter of Torah, who announces the conditions of blessedness (5:3–12) and interprets Torah in such fashion as to "fulfill" the law and prophets in a righteousness exceeding that of the Pharisees and scribes (5:17–20). The six antithetical statements in 5:21–47 exemplify his messianic interpretation of Torah as he responds to "what you have heard" with "I tell you . . ." in the boldest possible fashion. Matthew suggests by this pattern that Jesus knows precisely what God intended by the revelation of Torah and is now bringing God's original intention to light. The examples Matthew provides show a radicalization of Torah in three ways. In the case of murder and adultery (5:21–30), Jesus demands an *interior disposition* corresponding to outer action. For the prohibition of divorce and oath-taking (5:31–37), he demands an *absolute adherence* rather than a mitigating casuistry. In matters of human relationships (5:38–47), Jesus asks a *response that goes beyond* what the law requires.

Throughout the rest of the narrative, Matthew presents Jesus as the authoritative interpreter of Torah. In controversy stories, he has Jesus refer to the proper understanding of Torah (8:4; 12:12; 15:1–9). Jesus challenges his opponents' understanding of Torah—"Have you not read . . . ?"—following this challenge with a direct citation of Scripture (12:5; 19:4; 21:16, 42; 22:31). The opponents do not grasp that Jesus' deeds are actually his best interpretation of the true meaning of Torah: "Go and learn *(mathete)* what this is, 'I desire mercy and not sacrifice,' for I came not to call righteous people but sinners" (9:13; see also 12:7 and Hos. 6:6).

In Matthew's Gospel, Jesus is also shown to be the *fulfillment of Torah* in the specific details of his life. Matthew's characteristic way of making this point is through his use of a repeated formula to introduce explicit citations from Torah—citations that, as a kind of authorial commentary, he applies to Jesus: "This happened in order to fulfill the Scripture [or the saying of a prophet]." Matthew does this so consistently that the reader gains the sense that every aspect of Jesus' life conforms to Torah. Simply from these citations, we learn that Jesus is Immanuel, God with us (1:23; see Isa. 7:14) and that he is God's Son (2:15; see Hos. 11:1). We learn that he is a Nazarene (2:23; see Judg. 13:5; Isa. 11:1) but was born in Bethlehem as ruler of the people (2:6; see Mic. 5:2). His kingship was made manifest by his entry into Jerusalem (21:5; see Zech. 9:9). But he is also God's chosen Servant who bears the ills of others (8:17; see Isa. 53:4), a hidden Servant (12:18–21; see Isa. 42:1–4) who speaks in strange parables (13:35; see Ps. 78:2). He is betrayed by a companion for money (27:9–10; see Jer. 18:1–3). His significance is not only for Israel, because in his name the Gentiles will hope (12:18; see Isa. 42:1–4). For Galilee of the Gentiles, as for all nations (28:19), he is the great light that has dawned to shine on those who dwell in darkness (4:15–16; see Isa. 9:1–2).

Perhaps Matthew's boldest move is to suggest that Jesus also *personi-*

fies Torah. To grasp this aspect of his image of Jesus, we must remember some of the attributes of Torah in pharisaic Judaism. Wisdom had already been personified in Proverbs as the first of God's creations—with God in the beginning and also delighting to be among humans (8:4–31). The Wisdom of Solomon likewise personifies Wisdom as the reflection and image of God that passes from generation to generation into the souls of "holy people and prophets" (Wis. 7:25–27). The Book of Sirach in turn connects this personified Wisdom directly to Torah: "All this is the book of the covenant of the Most High God, the law which Moses commanded us" (Sir. 24:23, RSV). The Pharisees continued this identification. Those who studied Torah were the wise. Torah was with God from the beginning and had no end. Those who took its yoke upon them wore the yoke of the kingdom of God, which meant a share in God's own sabbath rest. The study of Torah mediated God's presence by means of the *Shechinah* (or "tenting/dwelling"): where two or three gathered in the study of Torah, there was the *Shechinah* present (*Sayings of the Fathers* 3.3). Such images provide a backdrop against which some of the statements placed in Jesus' mouth by Matthew take on a deeper resonance.

I have already suggested that when Jesus interprets Torah by stating, "I say to you . . . ," he assumes an authority that is astounding in Matthew's cultural context. He claims a virtual equality with Torah and the Giver of Torah. Matthew also has Jesus claim to be greater than the temple (12:6), greater than Jonah (12:41), and greater than Solomon (12:42). These comparisons also can be taken as asserting Jesus' superiority to the three parts of Torah: law, prophets, and writings. The suggestion cannot simply be dismissed, for Matthew has Jesus speak with the accents of a personified Wisdom: "I came not to call the righteous but sinners" (9:13). As Wisdom called people to life, so does he. And as Wisdom "delighted in the sons of men" (Prov. 8:31), so do we find Jesus defending himself when accused of consorting with sinners: "Wisdom is justified by her deeds" (11:19). And in his own voice, Jesus declares, "I will send out

153

prophets and wise men and scribes" (23:34). Jesus declares of Torah that its words will never pass away (5:18) but also says of his own words that they will never pass away (24:35), and he promises that he will be with his followers "until the close of the age" (28:20).

Such statements are provocative but not probative. Matthew provides two further sayings of Jesus, however, that cannot be taken except as suggesting that Jesus is the very personification of Torah. In contrast to the scribes and Pharisees, who place heavy burdens on people (23:4), Jesus—after identifying himself as the unique Son who can reveal the Father (11:25–27)—offers this invitation: "Come to me all who labor and are heavy burdened and I will give you rest. Take my yoke upon you and learn from me, for I am gentle and lowly in heart, and you will find rest for your souls; for my yoke is easy and my burden light" (11:28–30, RSV). Several aspects of this remarkably dense passage deserve comment. First, Jesus is identified as "gentle and lowly," and therefore embodying the qualities he prescribes as necessary for blessedness under the rule of God (5:5–3). Second, just as Torah revealed God's will to people, so does Jesus reveal the Father to whomever he wishes (11:27). Third, in contrast to the scribes and Pharisees—those "wise" from whom such revelation is hidden (11:25)—Jesus gives a light burden. Fourth, his "yoke" corresponds precisely with the symbol of Torah as "yoke of the kingdom." Fifth, as the Pharisees looked to Torah to learn God's ways, so are those who follow Jesus to "learn from me." Sixth, the commandment that more than any other distinguished Jews within society was the observance of the Sabbath, which was considered to be a participation in God's own sabbath rest; in this saying, "learning Jesus" brings such rest to the lives of his followers.

Finally, I return to the pharisaic premise that the *Shechinah* was to be present even among two or three who studied Torah together. We hear Jesus tell his disciples in 18:20, "Where two or three are gathered in my name, there I am among them." In Matthew's Gospel, Jesus is the teacher of Torah, the fulfillment of Torah, and the very personification of Torah.

Discipleship Within the Church

Matthew treats the disciples much more favorably than does Mark. This is in part because they do not, for him, represent all followers of Jesus, but only those chosen to hand on his teachings to the world (28:20). He is fond of the term "the twelve disciples" (10:1; 11:1; 20:17; 26:20), in effect identifying this group with the apostles (see 11:2, 5; 19:28; 26:14, 47). Because they must hand on Jesus' teachings to others, they must also have that "understanding" demanded by the "mysteries of the kingdom" spoken by Jesus; in this connection, notice in particular Matthew's explanation of the parable of the sower, in which "understanding" is the key to bearing fruit (13:19, 23). Matthew's disciples do in fact "see and hear" (13:10–17) what others do not, and do "understand all these things" taught by Jesus, and can therefore be "scribes educated for the kingdom of heaven" (13:51–52).

Matthew does not hide the hard facts of the disciples' moral inadequacy. Judas betrays Jesus, Peter denies him, and all the disciples abandon him, just as in Mark (26:56). Indeed, even at his appearance to the eleven disciples on the mountain, "some doubted" (28:17; see 14:31). But Matthew consistently softens the harshness of Mark's portrayal in such scenes as those of the stilling of the storm (8:23–27), the hemorrhaging woman (9:18–26), the transfiguration (17:1–8), and the second passion prediction, when the disciples are not "afraid" but only "greatly distressed" (17:23). Despite this softening, Matthew considers them morally flawed with respect to faith and loyalty: he has Jesus call them "people of little faith" (6:30; 8:26; 14:31; 16:8).

Matthew singles out Peter as the representative disciple for good and for ill. When Jesus walks on the water, in Matthew's version it is Peter who individually responds (14:18–31); Jesus' prediction of a future authority for the Twelve is given in response to a question from Peter (19:27–30); at Jesus' agony in the Garden of Gethsemane, Matthew makes it clear that it is Peter (not "Simon," as in Mark) who fails Jesus by sleeping (26:37, 40).

The positive and negative sides of Peter's role are shown in his confession and denial of Jesus. Peter shows "understanding" by giving much fuller recognition to Jesus' identity than we find in Mark's version: "You are the Messiah, the Son of the living God" (16:16). Jesus responds in kind, promising to Peter a place of authority in the church (16:17–19). Yet immediately after this, when Jesus predicts his suffering, Peter resists, saying, "May it be far from you, Lord " (16:22), and Jesus calls him "a stumbling block to me" (16:23). Likewise, with a small but telling detail, Matthew emphasizes the moral failing involved in Peter's denial of Jesus (26:69–75). As in Mark, Peter denies Jesus three times, but in two of his denials he takes a curse upon himself and swears (26:72, 74). Matthew thus shows that Peter rejected not only Jesus but also Jesus' teachings (see 5:34). Matthew fundamentally agrees with Mark, therefore, that his readers are not to look to the disciples as the models for their faith, but instead are to "learn from Jesus" (11:29).

I have mentioned the distinctive way in which Matthew inserts the term *church (ekklēsia)* into his narrative (16:18; 18:17). In one sense, all of Jesus' sayings in this Gospel are to be taken as the "commandments" by which the church is to live (28:20). Two of Jesus' discourses, however, focus on the life and activity of the community as such. Jesus sends the Twelve out on mission in 10:1–42. Like Mark, Matthew throws the shadow of rejection and persecution over this enterprise by placing the discourse in a section of his narrative where Jesus himself is also experiencing rejection (chaps. 8–12). The disciples too are therefore to expect rejection, persecution (10:14–25), and division within their households because of him (10:34–36). They should not fear in such circumstances, however, because Jesus will acknowledge the faithful before God (10:26–33). The disciples bear the authority to carry out the messianic tasks of preaching and healing (10:1, 7–8), and as his representatives they make the Messiah present. They can therefore expect the same reception and rejection that are his (10:40–42), for "a disciple is not above his teacher, neither is a slave above a master; it is enough for the disciple to be like his teacher, and the slave the master" (10:24 25). The postresurrection readers of Matthew's Gospel understand that these instructions pertain to them: the disciples are to continue to "embody" the Messiah in the world and are to follow in the same path of suffering that he walked.

In chapter 18, Matthew has Jesus address the church's communal life with a remarkable concentration on humility and service. Rebuke, correction, and even excommunication may be necessary for the messianic community, as they are for other communities that seek to live out a certain standard of behavior in the world. The church is not, however, to define itself in terms of the instruments of power. Greatness is measured by smallness, and the model for receiving the kingdom is a child (18:1–4). In similar fashion, the community as a whole is to show an active concern for "the little ones." They are to be received (18:5); they are not to be despised (18:10); they are not to be made to stumble (18:6–9). Instead, they are to be searched out and saved: "Thus is not the will of your father in heaven that any of such little ones should perish" (18:14).

Forgiveness is the characteristic note of life in the community in this Gospel (18:21–35; see also 6:12–15; 9:2–6). Yet if both discipline and forgiveness are necessary, the church is not yet the realized kingdom of God or an assembly of the perfect. The parable of the weeds with its interpretation (13:24–30, 37–43), the parable of the net and the fishes (13:47–50), and the parable of the wedding feast (22:11–14) all make it plain that a continual reform and response are required even for those in the church.

No parable makes it clearer that the community stands under judgment on the basis of its behavior than that of the sheep and the goats (25:31–46). The Son of man appears at the end of the ages to judge all the nations. The sole criterion for admission to the "kingdom prepared from the beginning of the world" (25:34) is not the confession of Jesus as Lord (see 7:21–23) but the way in which "one of the least of my brothers" was fed when hungry, given drink when thirsty, welcomed when a stranger, clothed when naked, and visited when sick and in prison (25:35–40). In the same way, the sole criterion for being sent to "the eternal fire made ready for the devil and his angels" (25:41) is not the failure to confess Jesus as Lord, but the failure to serve "the least of these my brothers" by feeding them when they were hungry, giving them drink when they were thirsty, clothing them when they were naked, welcoming them when they were strangers, and visiting them when they were sick or in prison: "Truly, I say to you, as you did it not to one of the least of these, you did it not to me" (25:42–46, RSV). The Torah of Jesus demands "mercy, not sacrifice" (12:7).

Matthew has deepened and expanded Mark's understanding of Jesus and of discipleship without fundamentally altering either. He has made the image of Jesus more complex by connecting Jesus more explicitly to the heritage of Israel (he is the personification of Torah) and the destiny of the church (he remains its teacher as risen Lord). Matthew has given more substance to the understanding of discipleship by showing how Jesus' teachings instruct both individuals and the church in what it means to "learn Jesus." No less than in James and in Paul, learning Jesus demands a life conformed to Jesus' own, lived in obedience to God and in service to others. At the end of Matthew's account of the Sermon on the Mount, Jesus declares,

> Not every one who says to me, "Lord, Lord" shall enter the kingdom of heaven, but the one who does the will of my Father in heaven. On that day, many will say to me, "Lord, Lord, did we not prophesy in your name and cast out demons in your name, and do many mighty works in your name?" And then I will declare to them, "I never knew you; depart from me you evildoers." (Matt. 7:21–23, RSV)

CHAPTER 10

Jesus in Luke-Acts

The evangelist we call Luke (perhaps a companion of Paul, perhaps not) also made good use of Mark's narrative when, in the latter part of the first century, he set out to improve on previous "narratives of the things brought to fulfillment among us" (Luke 1:1) for his Christian patron Theophilus, in order to "give him assurance concerning the things in which he had been instructed" (Luke 1:4). Like Matthew, Luke employs Mark's basic narrative spine from the baptism to the empty tomb, improving on the Greek as he goes, but respecting the substance and sequence of his source. Like Matthew, he adds discourse material from Q and from his own sources, but unlike Matthew, Luke distributes these sayings throughout the story rather than gathering them together in lengthy discourses.

Also like Matthew, he extends Mark's story by the addition of narrative material. In his Gospel, Luke attaches a prologue and an account of Jesus' early life (chaps. 1–2), as well as a complex set of resurrection appearance stories (chap. 24). His most extensive alteration, of course, is his addition of an entire second volume dealing with the birth and expansion of the church. This second volume—the Acts of the Apostles, or the Book of Acts—was quickly detached from the Gospel and placed in the New Testament canon before Paul's letters, but it was undoubtedly written as part of a single literary and theological project. Scholars today correctly read both volumes as part of a unitary composition that they term Luke-Acts. When we speak of "Luke's Gospel" in the sense of "what Luke set out to say about the good news God accomplished in Jesus," Luke-Acts as a whole (a full quarter of the New Testament canon!) is properly included in that discussion.

In Luke-Acts, the portrayal of Jesus and the drama of discipleship are opened up even further than they are in Matthew. Luke's account of Jesus and the origins of the church consciously sets out to write the continuation of the biblical story. Matthew had already placed Jesus in relation to Judaism and the church. Luke makes the Christian story a part of larger world history. He seeks to show how the story of Jesus and the church continues the story of Israel. Most of all, he wants to demonstrate that the inclusion of Gentiles in the people of God was also in fulfillment of God's promises, and that this entire narrative, when properly heard "in sequence" (Luke 1:3), confirms God's fidelity to his people. In so demonstrating, Luke produces the first Christian apology in the form of a historical narrative.

Jesus in the Plan of God

Luke's concern for telling his story "in sequence" affects his portrayal of Jesus. In Matthew and Mark, the postresurrection perspective of the evangelists finds implicit expression within their respective versions of Jesus' ministry. Because Luke has a second volume, the Book of Acts, in which to give full attention to the resurrection of Jesus and the sending of the Holy Spirit, he is better able to present the identity and mission of Jesus in stages. It is not that Luke's Gospel lacks a retrospective sense of Jesus' significance. On the contrary, readers understand the fuller significance of Jesus' being called "Son of God" at his annunciation (1:35) and the "Savior who is Christ the Lord" at his birth (2:11). They catch the point of Luke's concluding Jesus' genealogy with the sequence, "son of Adam, Son of God" (3:38), and the meaning of the voice from the cloud calling Jesus "beloved Son" at his baptism and transfiguration (3:22; 9:35).

But because he has the luxury of developing in the Book of Acts the full implications of Jesus' resurrection and enthronement, Luke is also able to allow Jesus' humanity room for expression in his first volume. And since Luke is concerned above all with defending the fidelity of God to the promises made to Israel, Jesus appears as one in a series of God's emissaries whose role it is to announce and fulfill those promises. What some observers have called Luke's "subordinationist" understanding of Jesus derives not from a desire to diminish Jesus' status but from a need to emphasize his role in working out God's plan. In Luke it is God who is the focus—who is in question, as it were—and in Luke it is God who gives the answer, because "God was with him" in all that Jesus did (Acts 10:38).

The Prophet Like Moses

In order to convey Jesus' role in God's plan for the salvation of the world, Luke draws on the image of the prophet. In Torah, the prophet is God's spokesperson who declares "the word of God" to the people in order to challenge them to a deeper commitment to the Lord. Because this word of God is addressed to specific social situations and structures, the prophet is also a figure who causes division among the people. Some accept the prophetic challenge and for that age form the "remnant people" of God; others reject the message and the messenger: the prophet is one who suffers and must look to God for vindication. This broad prophetic pattern perfectly fits Luke's understanding of Jesus.

Luke finds it most fully realized in the figure of Moses, who in Torah was regarded as the first and the greatest of the prophets. In the speech of Stephen before the Sanhedrin in Acts 7:17–44, Luke provides a sketch of the career of Moses the prophet. The speech reveals Luke's perception not only of Moses but also of the "prophet like Moses" whom God raised up— namely, Jesus of Nazareth (see Acts 3:22–23). According to Stephen, Moses was sent a first time to "visit his brethren the sons of Israel" and sought to intercede on behalf of an oppressed brother (7:24). Moses thought that they would recognize that "God was giving them deliverance by his hand," but "they did not understand" (7:25). As a result, they rejected Moses as their leader, forcing him into exile (7:26–29). In exile, however, Moses encountered God and was empowered to return to his people for a "second visitation" (7:30–34). This second time, Moses worked "signs and wonders" and brought the people out of Egypt (7:35–38). But the people rejected Moses a second time by turning to the worship of idols (7:39–41). The result of this rejection was not the exile of Moses but the exile of the people to Babylon (7:42–45).

Stephen's speech shows us the importance of Acts for interpreting Luke's narrative as a whole. The speech is not only about Moses but also about Jesus. First, Luke shows his readers that he wants them to make a connection between the two figures. In Acts 3:22–23, he has Peter declare to the crowd, "Moses said, 'The Lord your God will raise up for you a prophet like me from among your brothers. You will obey him in whatever he tells you. But every person that does not listen to that prophet will be destroyed from the people'" (see Deut. 18:19; Lev. 23:29). Then, in the midst of his story about Moses, Stephen says, "This is the Moses who said to the children of Israel, 'God will raise up for you a prophet like me from among your brothers'" (Acts 7:37).

Second, the story of Moses reveals that Luke understands the prophetic mission as one of bringing salvation to the people yet also involving suffering. Thus he has the risen Jesus say to his disciples, "'O foolish men and slow of heart to believe all that the prophets have spoken. Was it not necessary that the Christ should suffer these things and enter into his glory?' And beginning with Moses and all the prophets, he interpreted to them in all the scriptures the things concerning himself" (Luke 24:25–27, RSV).

Third, Stephen's description of Moses provides Luke with the pattern for his entire two-volume work. The first volume contains the first visitation of the prophet Jesus to Israel for their salvation, the rejection of him out of ignorance, and the beginning of his exaltation through resurrection. The second volume contains the completion of his exaltation and empowerment, and the "second visitation" of the people through Jesus' prophetic successors, the apostles. Filled with the Holy Spirit, the apostles work signs and wonders among the people "in the name of Jesus," offering a second chance at repentance. Those who accept become part of the remnant Israel that Luke describes in Acts 2:41–47 and 4:32–37. Those who reject the prophetic call are themselves rejected from the people.

The Prophetic Mission of Jesus

From the beginning, Luke prepares readers to perceive Jesus as a prophetic figure. The Holy Spirit overshadows his mother at his annunciation (1:35). Simeon prophesies that Jesus will be a sign of contradiction, causing the rise and fall of many in Israel (2:34). At his baptism the Holy Spirit comes on Jesus "bodily" (3:22). "Full of the Holy Spirit," he is "led by the Spirit" into the wilderness for testing (4:1), and he "returns in the power of the Spirit" (4:14). When Jesus reads from the prophet Isaiah in the synagogue of Nazareth, saying, "The Spirit of the Lord is upon me because he has anointed me to preach good news to the poor" (4:19; see Isa. 61:1–2; 58:6), readers already know the truth of Jesus' declaration to follow: "Today this scripture is fulfilled in your hearing" (4:21).

Jesus is the Anointed One of God, the Messiah. He will be called just that by Peter (9:20). He is anointed, however, not with oil but with the Holy Spirit. He is therefore a *prophetic* Messiah. Luke's construction of this inaugural scene enables it to function as a programmatic statement for the rest of Jesus' ministry. When Jesus subsequently proclaims, "Blessed are you poor" (6:20), it is in fulfillment of his prophetic charge. When in response to his wonders the people respond, "A great prophet has arisen among us. God has visited his people" (7:16), they recognize the truth about Jesus. When the voice from the cloud at the transfiguration alludes to Deuteronomy 18:19 by saying, "Listen to him" (9:35), Luke's readers are prepared to hear the other part of that verse applied to Jesus as the "prophet whom God has raised up" in Acts 3:22. And when Jesus' disconsolate followers declare after his death, "Jesus of Nazareth . . . was a prophet mighty in word and deed before God and all the people. . . . [W]e had hoped that he was the one to redeem Israel" (24:19–21), they also speak the truth that Luke has tried to convey in his narrative: Jesus is the prophet through whom God "visits the people" for their salvation (1:67).

Jesus' prophetic message is announced both through his speech and through his deeds. We notice that in Luke's interpretation of the parable of the sower, it is "the word of God" that is sown (8:11) and bears fruit among those who "hear the word and hold it fast in a good and true heart" (8:15). Jesus' "family" is made up of those who "hear the word of God and do it" (8:21). In Luke's Gospel, Jesus' mother, Mary, is in fact one who "hears and does" that word (1:38). Indeed, she is herself given a prophetic voice to announce how God's salvation will involve a reversal of human expectations: the rich and the poor will have their conditions exchanged, as will the weak and the powerful (1:51–52). The word of God spoken by Jesus the prophet is precisely the announcement of this reversal: the poor have good news proclaimed to them (4:18; 6:20; 7:22). Because "the poor" include all those who are dispossessed and oppressed and marginalized in human eyes, the prophet also announces "release to the captive, sight to the blind, liberty to those who are oppressed" (4:18), satisfaction to those who are hungry, laughter to those who weep (6:21), and forgiveness of sins to all (1:77; 4:18; 5:11–24; 7:47–49; 12:10; 17:3, 34; 23:24). The good news is that these "poor" are given a place in God's kingdom (6:20). Corresponding to this good news, however, is bad news for those who are now in positions of esteem and authority by human measure: "Woe to you that are rich . . . that are full . . . that laugh now . . . [that have] people speak well of you" (6:24–26).

Jesus embodies this prophetic message by his deeds. He not only "preaches the good news of the kingdom of God" (8:1), he also expresses God's powerful concern for those in need through his acts of healing and his gestures of communion. His healings are signs of God's power at work to "release" humans from their bondage to sin and all the ways in which sin works to imprison (2:24; 32). But he also associates with the outcast.

His prophetic ministry takes a different form than John's, but it generates no less division among the people:

> John the Baptist has come eating no bread and drinking no wine; and you say, "He has a demon." The Son of man has come eating and drinking, and you say, "Behold, a glutton and a drunkard, a friend of tax collectors and sinners!" (7:33–35, RSV)

Jesus' outreach to sinners shows God's desire to form a people from among those whom the world regards as unworthy. Jesus declares, "Healthy people don't need a doctor, sick people do. I have not come to invite righteous people to repentance, but sinners" (5:31–32), and again, "For the Son of Man came to seek and save what was lost" (19:10). The Lukan arrangement of materials in chapter 15 neatly attaches three parables of Jesus that perfectly express his ministry to the outcast—the lost sheep (15:3–7), the lost coin (15:8–10), and the lost son (15:11–32)—to the body language of acceptance with which Jesus enacted that ministry: "The Pharisees and scribes murmured, saying, 'This man wlecomes sinners and eats with them'" (Luke 15:1–3).

The prophet's call goes out to all without discrimination, but it does contain a demand for true repentance; what is required of all is the readiness to do works of justice, especially in regard to possessions. Luke uses the language of possessions to symbolize people's response to the prophetic call: "Whoever of you does not relinquish all that he has cannot be my disciple" (14:33). Those who respond positively are willing to follow Jesus' demand to leave their possessions (5:11, 27). Those who reject his prophetic message are characterized as "rich" and "lovers of money" (18:23; 16:14). But note that the wealthy tax collector Zacchaeus can express his repentance as he recognizes Jesus and invites him to his house: "Look, Lord, I am giving half of my goods to the poor. And if I have cheated anyone, I restore it fourfold," and Jesus responds, "Today salvation has come to this house, because he too is a child of Abraham" (19:8–9).

Within the Gospel narrative—especially in the long "travel" narrative of chapters 9–19, which shows the prophet heading toward his death in Jerusalem—Luke describes a people of God forming around the prophet Jesus. It is made up not only of those who are literally poor but also of those who are in any way marginal by the measure of that culture. Luke pays particular attention to the inclusion of sinners and women within this people (see 8:1–3). At the same time, those who are wealthy and powerful—represented in the story primarily by the leaders of the Jewish people—resist and reject the prophetic call to conversion.

The suffering of Jesus in Luke's Gospel is very much connected to this division that the prophet creates within the people. The challenge that Jesus poses to the established righteous and wealthy and powerful by his enacted message of God's favor to the poor and the outcast inevitably leads to conflict. Debates among his opponents concerning "what they might do to Jesus" (6:11) build in intensity (7:34, 39; 10:25; 11:16), escalating first to the desire to provoke him in order to "catch him at something he might say" (11:54) and then to an active attempt to destroy him (19:47). The Jewish leaders cooperate with Judas to have Jesus arrested (22:3–6), and they rig the charge against Jesus to accentuate its political threat to Rome (23:1–5). The continuing obtuseness of this leadership is expressed in the scene at the high priest's house, where "those holding him" subject Jesus to a cruel taunt—"Prophesy! Who is it that struck you?" (22:64)—little realizing that by rejecting the prophet Jesus they are themselves ironically fulfilling Scripture (see Isa. 52–53; Luke 22:37).

Luke makes two noteworthy alterations to the Markan passion account. The first can be seen in the shaping of the image of Jesus. In contrast to the almost raw suffering endured by Jesus in Mark's account, in Luke's version Jesus is markedly calmer and more self-possessed. At the Last Supper, he teaches his followers and bestows authority on them (22:24–38); in the Garden it is the disciples, not he, who are agitated (22:45); and as he goes through his time of testing he is comforted by an angel (22:43–44). He utters a prophecy over Jerusalem on the way to his crucifixion (23:26–31); then, at the site of the execution, he promises a place in his kingdom to one of those crucified with him (23:39–43), forgives his executioners (23:34), and dies with a verse from Psalm 31 on his lips, "Father, into your hands I entrust my spirit" (23:46). The centurion does not proclaim him as God's Son, but says, "Truly this was a righteous man" (23:47). As God's prophet, Jesus continues until the moment of his death to bear witness to God's fidelity.

The second major Lukan touch in the passion account concerns the people. In contrast to Matthew, who has all the populace claim responsibility for Jesus' death (Matt. 27:25), Luke exercises special care to exclude ordinary people from participation. In only one scene do they play a role, and their appearance there is so surprising that some scholars have sought to emend the passage (23:13). With that one exception, Luke consistently blames the rulers for the death of Jesus. At the cross, for example, it is not the whole populace that mocks Jesus, but only the leaders of the people (23:35–37). The populace stands by watching (23:35), but when they see how Jesus dies, they return to the city, beating their breasts in repentance (23:48). Luke effectively drives a wedge between those who were "hoping that Jesus would redeem Israel" and "the chief priests and rulers [who] delivered him up to be condemned to death and crucified him" (24:20–21). This same division continues in the account of Acts: the common people respond to the proclamation by the apostles of Jesus as raised prophet, while the leadership grows even more resistant in its rejection of the good news.

The Prophet God Has Raised Up

In the first chapter of this book, I showed how Luke develops the resurrection of Jesus in dialectical stages, using the narrative form to express aspects of Jesus' exaltation after death. The empty-tomb account (24:1–8) shows that Jesus is not among the dead but is "the Living One" (24:5); his appearances to the disciples express his real presence among them at meals and in surprising forms (24:13–49); his ascension (24:50–53; Acts 1:9–11) is a further degree of detachment from his former physical existence, preparing for a new form of presence through the Holy Spirit, expressed in the Pentecost account of Acts 2:1–5.

The second volume of Luke-Acts may indeed be read as an extended narrative argument concerning the power of Jesus' resurrection. The speeches that Luke places in the mouths of Peter and Paul provide the opportunity to elaborate the difference in the perception of Jesus given by his resurrection. We have seen in Matthew, for example, how the traditional messianic designation of "Son of David" is relativized by the understanding of Jesus as "Lord." In Acts, this comparison/contrast is worked out even more fully. The angel Gabriel tells Mary, before Jesus' birth, that God will give her son "the throne of his father David" (Luke 1:32). This promise is taken up by Peter in his Pentecost sermon:

> Brethren, I may say to you confidently of the patriarch David that he both died and was buried, and his tomb is with us to this day. Being therefore a prophet, and knowing that God had sworn with an oath to him that he would set one of his descendants upon his throne, he foresaw and spoke of the resurrection of the Christ, that he was not abandoned to Hades, nor did his flesh see corruption. This Jesus God raised up, and of that we are all witnesses. Being therefore exalted at the right hand of God, and having received from the Father the promise of the Holy Spirit, he has poured out this which you see and hear. For David did not ascend into the heavens; but he himself says, "The Lord said to my Lord, Sit at my right hand, until I make thy enemies a stool for thy feet." Let all the house of Israel therefore know assuredly that God has made him both Lord and Christ, this Jesus whom you crucified. (Acts 2:29–36, RSV)

The resurrection marks both continuity and discontinuity with Israel's past. Jesus is David's descendant, but in a way that David could not have imagined even as he prophesied it in his psalm. Jesus is not Messiah as the restorer of the land or even of the rule of Torah in the land. He is Messiah as one who shares the life of God—is "Lord" and has been given the Holy Spirit to share with other humans. This means also that the possession of this Holy Spirit—which Luke, like Paul, equates with the "promises to Abraham"—is the criterion of membership in the Israel constituted by this Messiah. As Peter declares in his next speech:

> You are the sons of the prophets and of the covenant which God gave to your fathers, saying to Abraham, "And in our posterity shall all the families of the earth be blessed." God, having raised up his servant, sent him to you first, to bless you in turning every one of you from your wickedness. (Acts 3:25–26, RSV)

Jesus is therefore "the prophet whom God has raised up"—"raised up" not simply in the sense of "chosen" but also in the sense of "being raised from the dead." Jesus' ascension into heaven does not mean his removal from the realm of human activity; it simply symbolizes the fact that his activity now takes another form than previously. Jesus can continue to be seen in visions and can speak authoritatively (Acts 7:54–55; 9:1–9; 22:17). Above all, however, his presence continues through the power of the Holy Spirit at work in the apostles. The Spirit that was at work in Jesus during his ministry (see 4:1, 16) is now at work in his followers, who continue his prophetic mission to the people, in fulfillment of the command of the risen Jesus:

> Thus it is written that the Christ should suffer and on the third day rise from the dead, and that repentance and forgiveness of sins should be preached in his name to all nations, beginning from Jerusalem. You are witnesses of these things. And behold, I send the promise of my Father upon you. (Luke 24:46–49, RSV)

The apostles, operating "in the name of Jesus," are therefore the prophet's "second visitation" of the people of Israel for their salvation. The

Israelites, who through their leaders and out of ignorance rejected Jesus (3:13–22), now have the chance to repent and to join the restored people of God that is being gathered by the power of this resurrected prophet.

Luke's concern in the first part of Acts is to show that the birth of the church is really the restoration of Israel, in fulfillment of God's promise. Despite the first rejection of the Messiah Jesus, Israel has been given a second chance through the preaching of the resurrected Lord Jesus. And many thousands of the Jews hear this good news, repent, and are baptized (2:41; 4:4; 6:7). As in Luke's first volume, it is the leadership that rejects the message from God and as a result is cut out of the people God is restoring (4:1–22; 5:17–42; 6:12–7:1; 8:1). When the good news is extended (through God's initiative!) to the Gentiles, then, it is not as a replacement for Israel but rather as an extension of the restored and messianic people. The "tent of David" having been restored, "the rest of humanity may seek the Lord and all the Gentiles who are called by my name" (Acts 15:16–17). Gentile readers like Theophilus, therefore—who might have grown insecure in their commitment to a God who could abandon the very people to whom he had made such promises—now understand, once the story is told in sequence, that God *did* remain faithful to Israel and is therefore a God in whom the Gentiles may entrust themselves "with assurance" (Luke 1:4).

Luke's portrayal of Jesus is therefore profoundly affected by the size and shape of his literary enterprise and his theological argument. Not the tightly focused drama of Messiah and disciples as in Mark, but the plan of God and the destiny of Israel form Luke's project. The image of Jesus as God's prophet is in service of Luke's effort to show that the significance of Jesus is for both Israel and the wider world of the Gentiles. The extension of Luke's narrative across two volumes allows him the opportunity to present the stages of Jesus' existence in his first visitation of the people and in the second visitation as resurrected Lord. The image of the prophet also enables Luke to focus on the social dimensions of Jesus' message: the announcement of God's good news means a reversal of human expectations and a realignment of human realities.

Despite the expanded framework for Jesus' mission, however, Luke's understanding of his identity and character is virtually identical to that of Mark and Matthew. As Jesus tells his disciples at the Last Supper, "I am among you as one who serves" (Luke 22:27). And although Acts naturally focuses on Jesus' exaltation and power, the importance of his suffering humanity by no means disappears. We find Philip overhearing the Ethiopian official reading from the prophet Isaiah:

> Now the passage of the scripture which he was reading was this: "As a sheep is led to the slaughter or as a lamb before its shearer is dumb, so he opens not his mouth. In his humiliation justice was denied him. Who can describe his generation? For his life is taken up from the earth" [Isa. 53:7–8]. And the eunuch said to Philip, "About whom, pray, does the prophet say this, himself or someone else?" Then Philip opened his mouth, and beginning with this scripture, he told him the good news of Jesus. (Acts 8:32–35, RSV)

In Acts we also find this wonderful summary of Jesus' ministry in Peter's speech to the Gentiles in Cornelius's household:

> You know the word he sent to Israel, preaching the good news of peace by Jesus Christ (he is the Lord of all), the word which was proclaimed throughout all Judea, beginning from Galilee after the baptism which John preached: how God anointed Jesus with the Holy Spirit and with power; how he went about doing good and healing all that were oppressed by the devil, for God was with him. And we are witnesses to all that he did both in the country of the Jews and in Jerusalem. They put him to death by hanging him on a tree; but God raised him on the third day and made him manifest; not to all the

people but to us who were chosen by God as witnesses, who ate and drank with him after he rose from the dead. (Acts 10:36–41, RSV)

The Chosen Witnesses

In each of the Gospels, readers learn Jesus—in the sense of being instructed in discipleship—not only from the way in which Jesus himself is depicted but also from the portrayal, for better or worse, of the disciples. We have observed that in the Gospels of Matthew and Mark, the image of the disciples corresponds to the portrayal of Jesus. Jesus as the mystery of the kingdom in Mark, for example, demands not understanding but fidelity in following the path of suffering he walks. In Matthew, Jesus as teacher of the church and personified Torah asks disciples to have an understanding heart as well as faithful obedience.

In Luke's two-part story, the disciples play still another role. They must function as Jesus' prophetic successors after his resurrection. Filled with the Holy Spirit, they will work signs and wonders as he did among the people, proclaiming the good news of salvation both to Israel and to the nations. They are to be, as Peter says, Jesus' "chosen witnesses." As in Matthew's Gospel, then, we should expect to see Luke soften Mark's harsh depiction of the disciples as stupid and disloyal. What is most intriguing about Luke's portrayal of the disciples in his first volume is the way they exemplify the positive response to Jesus' prophetic call. They are sinners (5:8, 32) who leave all their possessions in order to follow Jesus (5:11, 28; 18:28–30). Indeed, as they travel with him, they share their possessions (8:1–3) and participate in Jesus' feeding of the multitude (9:10–17). But they are not admirable in every respect. They grasp that Jesus is Messiah (9:20), but they consistently fail to grasp what Jesus means when he speaks of the need for the Messiah to suffer (9:44–45; 18:34) and of the need for them to give up their lives in order to follow him (9:23–25). It is this failure in understanding for which Jesus rebukes them in his resurrection appearances (24:25–27).

The disciples also reveal moral failures. They argue over who will be the greatest among them, not only during Jesus' ministry (9:46) but even at the Last Supper, after Jesus shares the bread and wine with them as symbols of his own service (22:24). They seek to husband authority to themselves (9:49–50) and punish those who do not receive them (9:54). As in Matthew and Mark, Judas betrays Jesus (22:3–5) and Peter denies him (22:54–62). Luke does not, however, note that all of the disciples flee when Jesus is arrested; and at the crucifixion, he notes, "all his acquaintances and the women who had followed him from Galilee stood at a distance and saw these things" (23:49).

In two places of the Gospel narrative Luke emphasizes the instruction of those who are to be Jesus' prophetic witnesses. In chapter 9, he clusters a series of scenes in which the disciples grasp part of who Jesus is but fail to grasp the implications of a servant Messiah. And at the Last Supper, Luke has Jesus promise the Twelve a role of authority over Israel (22:28–30) and instruct his followers more closely on the character of authority:

> The kings of the Gentiles exercise lordship over them, and those
> in authority over them are called benefactors. But not so with you.
> Rather let the greatest among you become as the youngest and the
> leader as one who serves. For which is the greater, the one who sits at
> table or the one who serves? Is it not the one who sits at table? But I
> am among you as one who serves. (22:25–27, RSV)

Finally, Jesus predicts both Peter's denial of him and his "turning" in order to strengthen his brethren (22:31–34).

In Acts we see Peter gathering the remnant disciples in order to interpret for them the defection of Judas and elect another witness of the ministry and resurrection of Jesus in preparation for the outpouring of the

Spirit promised by Jesus (1:15–26). Then, when the disciples are empowered by the prophetic Spirit (2:1–5), we see Peter bearing witness to Jesus as Messiah and Lord (2:14–36). The disciples now speak and act "in the name of Jesus" (3:6, 16; 4:30) with great boldness, such that even their opponents (knowing that the disciples are uneducated men) "[recognize] that they [have] been with Jesus" (4:13)! The apostles are Jesus' prophetic successors bearing witness to the people and, like Jesus, working "signs and wonders" in their midst (4:30; 5:12).

Luke shows that they learned their lessons from Jesus well. They exercise their authority over Israel in the midst of a community of possessions, seeing to the needs of widows (2:41–47; 4:32–37; 6:1–5) and continuing to "serve at tables" as Jesus did. They continue Jesus' prophetic proclamation of God's good news in the most radical manner imaginable, by extending inclusion in the people of God to the Gentiles and insisting on table fellowship with them (Acts 10–15). Most of all, they have clearly learned the lesson that such witnessing involves suffering in continuity with that of Jesus himself. Peter and John leave the council "rejoicing that they were counted worthy to suffer dishonor for the name" (5:41). Stephen suffers death at the hands of the Sanhedrin after accusing the assembly of "betraying and murdering the Righteous One" (7:52); at his death he sees Jesus at the right hand of God as the Son of man (7:56), but he dies in the manner Jesus did, forgiving his executioners (7:60) and praying, "Lord Jesus, receive my spirit" (7:59). When Paul in turn is converted, Ananias is told by Jesus in a vision, "He is a chosen instrument of mine to carry my name before the Gentiles and kings and sons of Israel; for I will show him how much he must suffer for the sake of my name" (9:16, RSV). And Paul with Barnabas makes the circuit of the churches they had founded, "strengthening the souls of the disciples, encouraging them to continue in the faith, and saying that through many tribulations we must enter the kingdom of God" (Acts 14:23). In the narrative of Acts, Luke provides a positive sketch of what following Jesus entails within the church, and what Jesus means by "Those who would come after me must deny themselves and take up their cross daily and follow me" (Luke 9:23, RSV).

In Luke-Acts, Jesus calls his followers to a participation in his own prophetic ministry. They are, like him, to challenge easy categories of separation and discrimination among people. They are, like him, to welcome the poor and outcast to the table of those who celebrate God's presence in the world and thus live within God's rule. They, like him, must be willing to face the suffering that such boldness in word and deed involves.

CHAPTER 11

Jesus in John's Gospel

The Fourth Gospel ultimately derives from an eyewitness designated as "the disciple whom Jesus loved" (John 13:23; 18:15–16; 19:26, 35; 20:2–10; 21:7, 20–23), but it also shows how that witness passed through a period of reflection in light of the church's postresurrection experience. No other Gospel, in fact, is so transparent concerning the ways in which the story of Jesus is read in light of the community's experience of his resurrection, the gift of the Holy Spirit, and the words of Scripture. In fact, John is so distinctive among the canonical Gospels that the best way to approach his rendering of Jesus may be through a comparison with the Synoptic witness of Matthew, Mark, and Luke.

John and the Synoptic Tradition

The first and most obvious difference is found in the facts of Jesus' ministry. John lacks the birth narratives of Matthew and Luke, although his prologue (1:1–18) serves a similar function of situating Jesus—"who was made flesh and dwelt among us" (1:14)—with regard to God, the world, the Jewish tradition, and those who believe in him:

> The true light that enlightens every man was coming into the world. He was in the world, and the world was made through him, and the world did not know him. He came among his own, and his own people did not receive him. But to all who received him, who believed in his name, he gave power to become children of God. (1:10–13)

The Synoptics all sketch a one-year active ministry of Jesus that begins and centers in Galilee, moving to Jerusalem only for Jesus' climactic death. In John, on the other hand, Jesus moves back and forth between Judea and Galilee. He appears first in Judea but then goes to Galilee (1:28, 43). He makes a brief trip to Jerusalem for the Passover feast (2:13) and while there purifies the temple (2:13–22), an event that the Synoptics place at the end of his career. Jesus then goes from Jerusalem to Judea (3:22) and from Judea back to Galilee through Samaria (4:3, 45), returning to Jerusalem for another feast (5:1). He spends another Passover in Galilee (6:4) but goes to Jerusalem again for the Feast of Booths (7:1–10), and he is still there for the Feast of the Rededication of the Temple (10:22). He then returns to Judea (10:40), where he sojourns until his final Passover in Jerusalem (12:12). This review indicates three ways in which John's presentation differs from the Synoptics: Jesus' work centers in Judea rather than Galilee, it lasts three years rather than one, and events cluster around the great pilgrimage feasts of Judaism.

Even the circumstances of Jesus' death and resurrection are different in John's Gospel: Jesus is crucified on the day of preparation for the Passover in John (19:31), so that his final meal is not a Passover celebration as it is in the Synoptics; and while a meal is presupposed, it is not described. Instead, the foot-washing of the disciples is the ritual act prescribed for them to imitate (13:5–15). John mentions that Jesus is anointed before his burial (19:39–42), an element missing from the Synoptics. In John's account it is Mary Magdalene who goes alone to the tomb and finds Jesus missing (20:1) before reporting to Peter and John, who then run to the tomb (20:2–10). Jesus appears once to Mary alone after the resurrection (20:11–18) and twice to the disciples in Jerusalem (20:19–29). He bestows the Holy Spirit on them and commissions them (20:20–23), but there is no "ascension and Pentecost" in John as there is in Luke-Acts. Jesus' sole postresurrection appearance in Galilee is on the seashore rather than on Matthew's mountaintop (21:1–14). It is impossible, in short, to fully harmonize the facts of Jesus' ministry, death, and resurrection in the Fourth Gospel and the Synoptic Gospels.

Even more striking is John's presentation of Jesus' characteristic modes of acting and speaking. There are, for example, no exorcisms in this Gospel, even though exorcisms are critical for the Synoptics' portrayal of Jesus' victory over evil powers. Furthermore, Jesus performs only three healings and one resuscitation in John's Gospel. Although the healings involve "an official's son" (4:46–54), a "paralytic" (5:2–9), and a "blind man" (9:1–8)—figures who also appear in healings in the Synoptics—the healings are in each case different. Likewise, the resuscitation in John involves Jesus' friend Lazarus (11:38–44) rather than the widow of Naim's son (Luke 7:11–16). In John's account, these actions of Jesus all take place in the period of Jesus' open ministry (chaps. 1–12); called "signs" *(sēmeia)*, they generate belief among his followers and controversy among his opponents.

Jesus' words, in turn, bear little resemblance to those reported in the Synoptic Gospels. Jesus tells none of the parables found in the other Gospels and speaks only a handful of "figures" (10:6; 16:25). In the Synoptics, Jesus' speech tends toward the aphoristic; in John, it characteristically takes the form of discourse. In the Synoptics, Jesus' controversies with opponents are short vignettes that end with a pronouncement; in John, the controversies are extended and turn into monologues: it is not so much the deeds of Jesus as the claims implicit in them that become the issue for debate (see 5:10–47; 6:41–65; 9:35–10:39).

John's Gospel does share material concerning Jesus that is also found in the Synoptics. The sequence in which Jesus multiplies the loaves and walks on the water (John 6:1–21) is particularly close to the version found in Mark 6:34–51. The Fourth Gospel also includes John's baptism (1:25; 3:23) and arrest (3:24; see Mark 1:4, 14), Peter's confession of Jesus (6: 68–69; Mark 8:29), the purification of the temple (2:14–16; Mark 11:15–18), the anointing at Bethany (12:1–8; Mark 14:3–9), and the entry into Jerusalem (12:12–15; Mark 11:9–10). Above all, John includes the passion account (18:1–19:42), which—although it has its distinctive elements, such as the role played by Pilate (18:29–19:22)—is recognizably the same as in the Synoptics, agreeing most closely with Luke's version.

Thematic elements that the Synoptics compress into single incidents are found diffused through the Fourth Gospel. The Synoptic temptation account (Matt. 4:1–11), for example, finds an equivalent in John 6:14–15 and 7:3–4, while the agony in the Garden (Mark 14:32–42) is matched by John 12:27–29 and 18:11. It is even possible to discern the reworking of some Synoptic sayings material in passages such as John 1:42, 12:24–26, 13:12–20, and 21:22. But it must be stated simply: most of what is in John is not in the Synoptics, and most of what is in the Synoptics is not in John. This is a distinctively different narrative rendering of the good news.

The Distinctive Character of John

The Fourth Gospel gains its special character by being a theological reflection in the form of a story. We have seen that the witness of the other Gospels does not lack interpretation, but in John the interpretive element is so impressive that the very narrative takes on a meditative tone. The story appears less as a linear recital of events than as a reflective consideration of the deeper significance of those events. The explicitly theological dimension of this Gospel can be seen in four features.

John is an ecclesiastical Gospel. Although this narrative never uses the word *church* and tells us nothing about church organization, no other Gospel so consistently connects the events concerning Jesus to the community of readers and the narrator's perspective. Notice the self-consciousness revealed in the narrator's statement of purpose in writing (20:30–31), in the way Jesus' future presence among believers is promised before his death (14:25–31; 15:1–11), and above all in the acknowledgment that deeper insight into Jesus came about as a result of the gift of the Holy Spirit after the resurrection (2:17–22; 7:37–39; 12:16; 14:25; 20:9). Because the reader is explicitly told of the influence of this later perspective, John is free to collapse the chronological distance between the story of Jesus and the experience of believers. He recognizes the difference between the two times (14:15–30; 16:7–15, 19–28, 31–33), but the reality of the present is allowed to permeate the narration of the past. The signs worked by Jesus are recognizable as the church's own signs; the misunderstanding faced by Jesus is the misunderstanding experienced by the church (3:11); the conflicts generated by Jesus are those of the community as well (9:22; 12:42): "If the world hates you, it hated me first" (15:18).

John is also a sacramental Gospel. The only institution of a ritual by Jesus in John, as I have mentioned, is the foot-washing at his last meal (13:1–14). But John's Gospel is permeated by an awareness of other ritual traditions. The figure of Jesus is interpreted against the backdrop of the Jewish feasts of Passover, Booths, and Hanukkah. The symbolism of these feasts is attached to Jesus: he is the living bread (6:51), the living water (4:14; 7:37–39), the light of the world (8:12), and the lamb of God who bears the sins of the world (1:29; 19:36). But the Gospel also shows an awareness of the Christian sacraments of baptism and the eucharist, rooted both in these Jewish feasts and in the transformation of them in the person of Jesus (2:1–11; 3:5; 4:14; 6:35–58; 7:37–39; 19:34).

John's Gospel has a distinctive eschatology that is connected with its sense of the life of the church. There are statements concerning the expectation of a future resurrection and judgment involving Jesus (5:28–29; 11:24). But the Gospel's main emphasis is that the end-time is in some sense present already in the figure of Jesus and in the experience of believers: "The time is coming and now is" (4:23; 5:25). John does not suggest that believers are living a heavenly life, but rather that already in Jesus the definitive offer of life and the critical judgment of the world have occurred. Jesus is "the resurrection and the life" (11:25), and people are judged on the basis of their response to him (5:25–27). Those who believe in him can be called "children of God" (1:12) and claim a share in eternal life: "This is eternal life, that they know you the only true God and Jesus Christ whom you sent" (17:3).

These first three aspects of John's theological sensibility find their focus in the figure of Jesus himself, who in John appears as much a symbolic as a literal figure. I do not mean by this that Jesus is not understood by John to be fully human—rather, that the narrative role assigned him makes his literary representation necessarily more than literal. This is to some extent the case in the other Gospels as well: Mark's Jesus is scarcely just another Jewish teacher, for example. In John's Gospel, however, the depiction of Jesus as "God's Word" is so powerful that it has sometimes been thought to overshadow John's insistence that this Word was also "made flesh and dwelt among us" (1:14).

In fact, however, John's Jesus is in some ways even more fully rounded in his humanity than the Jesus portrayed by the Synoptics. Jesus is shown experiencing fatigue (4:6) as well as anguish (12:27; 13:21). His whole being is convulsed when he contemplates the death of his friend Lazarus, and he weeps (11:33–35). On one occasion he changes his mind (7:1–10). He converses with real people in real and identifiable places. His conversation with the Samaritan woman, for example, is distinctive, not exchangeable with any other (4:7–26). Rather than issuing punchy one-liners, he enters into conversational exchanges with Nicodemus (3:1–13), the paralytic (5:2–9), the man born blind (9:35–38), his friends Martha and Mary (11:17–37), and his disciples (1:38–51; 4:31–38; 6:66–71; 9:1–5; 11:1–16; 13:31–14:31). His controversies with opponents do not end quickly but demand his continued engagement (6:41–65; 7:14–36; 8:12–58; 10:22–39). This Jesus performs a miracle simply for the pleasure of giving pleasure (2:1–11). He shows irritation (2:4; 6:26; 7:6–8; 8:25) and suspicion (2:24–25). He asks for a positive human response (6:66–71). Jesus has real friends and is involved in their lives (11:1–12:9). He has one disciple whom he loves more than the others (13:23; 19:26; 20:2; 21:20). He cares about his mother (2:1–11) and seeks her welfare before he dies (19:26–27). He asks of Simon three times, "Do you love me more than these?" (21:15–17). And he designates his followers simply as "friends" (15:13–15). This is a thoroughly human Jesus; Christians throughout the ages who have loved the humanity of Jesus in John's Gospel have not been mistaken in their reading.

How, then, do we account for the other aspect of John's portrayal of Jesus—the aspect that makes him appear to be something more than human, speaking "as no man has ever spoken" (7:46)? That aspect is the logical result of the theological dimension of John's narrative, discussed above. In that dimension, John makes explicit the claims that lie implicit within the Synoptics. When Jesus proclaims in Mark 1:15, "The time is fulfilled, the kingdom of God is at hand, repent and believe the good news," his statement explicitly concerns God's rule, but implicit within it are a number of claims concerning Jesus and his relationship to that rule: that he is God's spokesperson, that he knows the plan of God, that in his preaching the goal of history is being reached. What gives John's Gospel its distinctive character is that it makes such implicit claims explicit. The whole drama of God's relationship with humanity is played out in this Gospel, with Jesus as the central character. John's is the most consistently Christocentric of the Gospels, and for this reason Jesus appears as a more symbolic than literal figure. He bears the narrative burden of revealing God in the world.

Jesus Reveals God

The prologue to John's Gospel sets the framework within which the reader perceives Jesus. In Jesus, the eternal Word that was with God in the beginning and through which the world came into being (1:1–3) came into the world as God's own light, challenging humans to see the world in this light or to remain in darkness (1:9–12). This Word became flesh, and in him could be seen "glory as of the only Son from the Father" (1:14). The prologue's ending perfectly summarizes the literary and theological function of Jesus in the narrative: "No one has ever seen God; the only-begotten Son [or, in another reading, "God"], who is in the bosom of the Father, he has made him known" (1:18). The Greek verb that is translated "has made him known" *(exēgēsato)* contains the sense both of revealing and of interpreting. Jesus makes known and interprets God in his very humanity. If a symbol is defined as a sign that participates in that which it signifies, then Jesus in his humanity is the symbol of God in the world.

It is for this reason also that his miracles are called "signs" in this Gospel. Giving sight to the blind points to the light of the world, giving bread to the multitude points to the true bread from heaven, and changing water into wine points to the power of creation: these deeds point to the power of God that Jesus makes present in the world.

Each of the Gospels uses the names given to Jesus by various characters to provide access to aspects of his identity. In John, that process of naming is particularly complex, beginning already with the call of the disciples, each of whom applies to Jesus one of various traditional Jewish titles—"Lamb of God," "Rabbi," "Messiah," "Son of God," "King of Israel" (see 1:29–51). Apart from the charge made by his opponents that he was a Samaritan and had a demon (7:20; 8:48), everything said about Jesus in the Fourth Gospel has some element of truth. But as we move from the designations assigned by outsiders to those assumed by Jesus himself, we see that some characterizations are more adequate than others.

The traditional titles applied to Jesus by outsiders—"Messiah," "prophet," "king"—demonstrate John's use of literary irony: the author and readers understand the truth of what is said in a way different than do the characters who speak. Christian readers grasp how Jesus both fulfills and exceeds traditional expectations associated with these titles. We see Jewish leaders and the disciples inquiring whether John might be the Messiah or a prophet (1:20, 21, 25; 3:28), the Samaritan woman at the well wondering whether Jesus is the Messiah (4:29), and a crowd in Jerusalem wondering if the leaders might secretly know that Jesus is the Messiah (= Christ; 7:26). These speculations reveal then-current perceptions of the Messiah in Judaism: that he would be from Bethlehem (7:42), or that his origin would be unknown (7:27); that he would perform great signs (7:31), reveal all things (4:25), and remain forever (12:34). Jesus' opponents, of course, think that Jesus does none of these things. But the reader has been told by the narrator that Jesus does reveal all things, does perform great signs, does have an origin in God hidden from human view, and will "remain forever." The titles "prophet" (4:19; 6:14; 9:17) and "king" (6:15; 18:33–39; 19:12–22), which were associated with the "prophet like Moses" who would restore Israel, likewise operate on two levels—Christian readers understand Jesus to be prophet as the one who reveals God, and king not only of the Jews but of all humans seeking the truth about God: "You say that I am a king. I was born for this and for this I have come into the world, in order to bear witness to the truth. Every one who is of truth hears my voice" (18:37).

These traditional titles used by outsiders are not wrong when used by believers, but for people of faith they require supplementation by a deeper insight into Jesus' identity. Thus Jesus is called "Messiah" also by those coming to belief in him (1:41; 11:27)—a designation certified as appropriate both by Jesus himself (17:3) and by the narrator, who writes (he explains) so that readers may continue to believe that Jesus is "the Christ, the Son of God" (20:31). The title "Son of God," however, provides a deeper understanding of the traditional role of Messiah. Thus Nathaniel also calls Jesus "Son of God, King of Israel" (1:49), and John the Baptist calls Jesus "Son of God" (1:34). Martha represents all believers when she confesses, "I believe that you are the Christ, the Son of God, the one who is coming into the world" (11:27) in a cluster of attributes fully in agreement with the prologue (see 1:9, 14, 17). Peter likewise calls Jesus "the Holy One of God" (6:69). The Fourth Gospel even uses the title "God" *(Theos)* for Jesus, though only sparingly. We find it first in the prologue's "the Word was God" (1:1), and possibly in "the only God who was in the bosom of the Father, he has made him known" (1:18, variant reading). When Thomas confesses Jesus at a resurrection appearance as "my Lord and my God" (20:28), therefore, he is not out of line with the evangelist's own view of Jesus' identity.

The most intimate access to Jesus' identity in John's Gospel is provided by Jesus' own self-designations. In the three Synoptic Gospels, the title "Son of man" is used with reference to Jesus' present authority, his suffering, and his future role as judge. In John, the title is used only once (out of many occurrences) as a simple self-designation: "Do you believe in the Son of man?" (9:35). But as in its first occurrence (1:51), the dominant usage of that title is within a pattern of descent and ascent: Jesus is the one who will be "lifted up" in his crucifixion (3:14; 8:28), which is also his exaltation (13:31); when he is lifted up, the Son of man will draw all people to himself (12:32–34) so that they may have eternal life (3:15). But this Son of man is also one who has already "descended" by coming from God. He is the man from heaven who is uniquely capable of revealing the things "from above" (3:12, 31; see 8:23). When this Son of man is "lifted up," it is to return to where he was before (6:62). Since for this Gospel "no one has seen the Father except the one who is from God, he has seen the Father," the Son of man language establishes a pattern of descent and ascent that validates Jesus as both revealer and judge: "No one has ascended into heaven but the one who descended from heaven, the Son of man" (3:13; see 5:27). The use of title "Son of man" is a fascinating example of the way in which John shares the Synoptic tradition at a deep level but gives it his own distinctive turn.

Unique to the Fourth Gospel are statements made by Jesus using the phrase "I am" *(ego eimi)*. Seven of these statements are basically metaphorical and take the form of an implied comparison to something already known, of which Jesus represents the authentic realization. Beneath the metaphor is also the claim to be the source of that life *(zōē)* that comes only from God. After multiplying the loaves, for example, Jesus declares, "I am the bread of life" (6:35, 48), in contrast to the manna Moses gave in the desert, which was not really "bread from heaven" (6:32). Only Jesus can be the genuine bread (6:35); he descends from God and offers the life that comes from God, "for the bread of God is the one who comes from heaven and gives life to the world" (6:33). A similar pattern of contrast is found in Jesus' statements "I am the light of the world" (8:12; 9:15), "I am the door of the sheep" (10:7), "I am the good shepherd" (10:11), and "I am the true vine" (15:1).

The metaphorical aspect is diminished in two final examples, which suggest simply that Jesus *is* what the other metaphors suggest: the source of life. In response to the crisis of Lazarus's death and Martha's statement of belief in a future resurrection (11:24), Jesus declares, "I am the resurrection and the life" (11:25). And at the Last Supper, Jesus tells his followers, "I am the way and the truth and the life; no one comes to the Father except through me" (14:6). This statement makes clear what all the rest have suggested: in contrast to every form of human striving, Jesus brings the authentic life that comes from God. He is revealer and life-giver.

Jesus also uses "I am" absolutely. On several occasions, this is simply a matter of identification to an interlocutor (see 4:26; 6:20), but even these utterances may hold a deeper resonance (see, e.g., 18:5–6). The most telling usage is in Jesus' disputation with Jewish opponents in 8:12–58, where it occurs three times. Jesus tells his opponents, "You will die in your sins unless you believe that *ego eimi,*" and they naturally ask, "Who are you?" (8:24–25). A second time he says to them, "When you have lifted up the Son of man, then you will know that *ego eimi*" (8:28). Finally, Jesus tells them that Abraham has seen him. When his opponents mock, Jesus responds, "Truly truly, I say to you, before Abraham was, *ego eimi*" (8:58). That the opponents recognize the deeper implications of this self-designation is shown by their picking up stones to throw at him for blasphemy (8:59). Later they will state that they wanted to stone him because, "although a human being, he makes himself God" (10:33). This is exactly what the absolute use of *ego eimi* would suggest. The opponents (and the

Gospel's readers) recognize in this strange locution an echo of God's self-identification to Moses in the burning bush—"I am who I am" (Exod. 3:14)—and the divine self-designation of "I am" in the prophet Isaiah (Isa. 41:4; 43:10).

The deepest level of self-revelation in the speech of Jesus is found in his use of filial language for his relationship with God. The narrator tells us that Jesus was sent into the world as an only-begotten Son (1:18; 3:16–17). Jesus himself says that just as human sons observe their fathers working, so can he do nothing of himself but only what he observes his Father doing: he works as his Father works (5:19). This means that he carries out in the world the same functions as God. As the Father is the source of life, so also does the Son have this life in him (5:21), which he can give to others (5:26; 6:40, 57). The Son is a judge just as the Father is a judge (5:22) and deserves to receive honor just as the Father receives honor (5:23). It is as his Father's Son that he bears witness (5:30); he hears the words spoken by the Father and in turn speaks them to the world. He is, therefore, an obedient Son (8:26–28). The Father, in turn, loves the Son (3:35; 5:20) and gives him glory (8:54; 12:28). The blindness of Jesus' opponents to his real identity can be summarized in the words, "They did not know he spoke the Father to them" (8:27). Similarly, Jesus can say to his disciples, "The one who has seen me has seen the Father" (14:9). In the language of this filial relationship characterized by obedience and love, Jesus provides the inner meaning of the designation "only Son of God" (1:14, 18).

It is in Jesus' words to his followers at his final meal that the fullest and most explicit revelation of Jesus' role as revealer of the Father occurs. From the beginning of the Gospel, readers are told that the "hour" for Jesus' "glorification" has not yet arrived (2:4; 7:30; 8:20). But at the end of his public ministry, Jesus declares that "the hour has come for the Son of man to be glorified" (12:23). The hour of Jesus' glorification is the period of his suffering, death, and resurrection: this is the "lifting up of the Son of man" that will represent at once Jesus' return to the God who sent him and the bestowal of the Spirit on his followers. In these final moments before his arrest, the reader is told plainly and explicitly that Jesus is going away to the Father from whom he came (13:1, 3, 33, 36; 14:3, 12, 19, 28, 30; 16:5–7; 17:11, 13). Jesus himself declares, "I came from the Father and have come into the world; again, I am leaving the world and am going to the Father" (16:28). He thus becomes also the way by which others can go to the Father (14:4–7). The relationship between Jesus and the Father is one of the greatest intimacy: he and the Father are one (14:8–11; 16:15; 17:21). While Jesus is not the Father, he remains united with God through obedience and love (14:10, 31; 15:9, 15; 17:4, 12, 13).

The Expression of Obedience and Love

John's emphasis on the fact that Jesus reveals God might be taken—indeed, *has* been taken by some readers—as an implicit slighting of Jesus' humanity. All the revelatory discourse seems to them ultimately to be empty: Jesus' revelation is simply and exclusively that he is the revealer. But this sort of reading misses the significance of the narrative form adopted by John, in which Jesus not only speaks but also acts. In his human activity, Jesus reveals his character as obedient Son and provides specific content to his identity as revealer of God.

I have already suggested that John seeks to show the humanity of Jesus through multiple and real human relationships. Likewise, in John all of Jesus' miracles except walking on the water are expressions of human care and compassion, and therefore serve as signs of the life-giving power from God active in Jesus. They also express the truth that what Jesus says and does as "Savior of the world" (4:42) is in obedience to God and in service to humans.

Jesus tells Nicodemus that "God so loved the world that he gave his only Son that whoever believes in him should not perish but have eternal life" (3:16, RSV). As God's gift to the world for its salvation, Jesus does everything out of obedience to the Father: "My food is that I do the will of the one who sent me and that I complete his work" (4:34). Jesus always does what is pleasing to the Father (8:29): "I have come down from heaven not to do my own will but the will of the one who sent me, and this is the will of him who sent me, that I lose nothing of all that he has given to me, but raise it up on the last day" (6:36–39, RSV). So when Jesus confronts the hour of his death, he says, "Now my soul is troubled. And what shall I say? 'Father save me from this hour'? But for this I have come to this hour. Father, glorify thy name!" (12:27–28). Jesus' passage to death in John's Gospel is one of total and faithful obedience. At the cross, he does not cry out in agony. Instead, knowing that he has brought all the Scripture to fulfillment (19:28), he says, "It is finished," and bowing his head, gives up his spirit (19:30).

John also makes it clear that Jesus' life of obedience is one of service to others. The entire meaning of his human life is to be that "lamb of God who bears [or: takes away] the sins of the world" (1:29, 33). Jesus' death is salvific not only for Israel but for all humans (11:50–52; see 4:42). In contrast to the hireling shepherds who look out only for themselves and flee when the sheep are in danger, Jesus is "the good shepherd. The good shepherd lays down his life for the sheep" (10:11). The intense level of intimacy between Jesus and his own people, as well as the level of intentionality attributed to Jesus by this Gospel, is well expressed in the development of this image:

> I am the good shepherd. I know my own and my own know me, as the Father knows me and I know the Father. And I lay down my life for the sheep. And I have other sheep that are not of this fold. I must bring them also and they will hear my voice. So there shall be one flock, one shepherd. For this reason the Father loves me, because I lay down my life, that I may take it up again. No one takes it from me, but I lay it down of my own accord. I have power to lay it down

and I have power to take it up again. This charge I have received from my Father. (10.14–18, RSV)

Jesus' death and resurrection are to be the source of life for others: "Truly, truly I tell you, unless the grain of wheat falls into the ground and dies, it remains alone; but if it dies it bears much fruit" (12:24). John symbolizes this pattern in another way at the crucifixion. In the moment before "giving up his spirit" (19:30), Jesus says, "I thirst" (19:28), yet when his side is lanced by the soldier, blood and water come forth (19:34). John wants his readers to understand that from the self-emptying thirst of Jesus comes the gift of the Spirit, so he recalls the prophecy of Jesus:

If anyone thirst, let him come to me and drink, the one who believes in me. As the Scripture has said, "Out of his heart shall flow rivers of living water." (Now this he said about the Spirit, which those who believed in him were to receive; for as yet the Spirit had not been given, because Jesus was not yet glorified.) (7:38–39, RSV)

Learning Jesus in John

As in the other Gospels, the disciples of Jesus play a key role in the narrative and serve as a point of identification for readers who now see themselves also as "following Jesus." In general, it can be said that just as John elevates the figure of Jesus, so does he improve the character of the disciples, especially of the Twelve "whom he chose" (6:70). It is in the face of apostasy by other disciples after Jesus' discourse on the living bread, for example, that Peter speaks for the Twelve: "Lord, to whom shall we go? You have words of eternal life; and we have come to believe and know that you are the Holy One of God" (6:68). Coming to believe and to know: that is the first stage of discipleship for John, who writes his Gospel so that readers might continue in such belief (20:30–31).

John does not deny the moral deficiency of the disciples: Judas is corrupt (12:6) and betrays Jesus (6:70–71; 13:2, 28–30; 18:2–3); Peter denies Jesus (18:17, 25–27). But in the main they do what Jesus most asks—namely, "remain with him" (1:38–39; see 15:4–11). Thus Thomas is willing to die with Jesus by going with him to Lazarus's side (11:16). Joseph of Arimathea risks retribution by seeking the body of Jesus after his death, and with Nicodemus buries Jesus (19:38–40). Above all, "the disciple whom Jesus loved" proves to be faithful throughout. He follows Jesus after his arrest in the company of Peter (18:15–16), but unlike Peter does not deny Jesus. John stands at the cross of Jesus together with Jesus' mother, Mary the wife of Clopas, and Mary Magdalene—as in the Synoptics, the women are not called disciples but are more impressive for their loyalty and courage than the official males designated by that term—and Jesus entrusts his mother to this disciple (19:26–27). The beloved disciple is an eyewitness to the death of Jesus (19:35) and is the first witness to the resurrection: "The other disciple who reached the tomb first also went in, and he saw and he believed" (20:5). He is also the first to recognize Jesus when he appears to the disciples in Galilee: "It is the Lord!" (21:7). It is his unexpected death that must be explained to a community that had thought he would live until Jesus' return (21:23). Clearly, for the readers of John's Gospel, the beloved disciple represents the ideal follower of Jesus.

As in the Synoptics, however, Peter remains a more ambiguous and therefore more intriguing figure. At the last meal he plaintively asks, in response to Jesus' declaration that where he is going they cannot now follow, "Lord, why am I not able to follow you now? I will lay down my life for you." Jesus answers by predicting his denial (13:36–38). After his denial, Peter disappears from the story until the empty-tomb account: then he runs with the beloved disciple to the tomb in response to Mary Magdalene's message concerning the removal of the body, but he is not said to come to belief (20:1–10). When Jesus appears in Galilee and is recognized by the beloved disciple, Peter jumps from the boat into the water—it is not said in what direction (21:7). Yet Peter is singled out by Jesus at the end as the disciple who, loving him more than the others, is to "tend the sheep" for him (21:15–17). And Jesus prophesies that Peter too will "glorify God" by his death. In the meantime, Jesus says to Peter, "Follow me" (21:19). And when Peter inquires into the destiny of the beloved disciple, Jesus rebuffs him and repeats, "Follow me" (21:22).

As in the Synoptics, so in John: those who seek to "learn Jesus" follow him by conforming their lives to the pattern of his. The Holy Spirit breathed on them by the resurrected Jesus gives them the authority to forgive as he forgave (20:22–23). It also dwells in them (14:17), leading them into a fuller understanding of the meaning of Jesus' words and deeds (14:25–26) and guiding them into all truth (16:12–15). They are thus able to understand the foot-washing (13:5–11) as an embodied parable of Jesus' entire existence:

> Do you know what I have done to you? You call me Teacher and Lord; and you are right, for so I am. If I then, your Lord and Teacher, have washed your feet, you also ought to wash one another's feet. For I have given you an example, that you should also do as I have done to you. Truly, truly, I say to you, a servant is not greater than his master; nor is he who is sent greater than he who sent him. If you know these things, blessed are you if you do them. (13:12–17, RSV)

Such a life of service is directly connected by John to the pattern of Jesus' self-disposition. After the saying on the grain of wheat that must die, Jesus continues:

> He who loves his life loses it, and he who hates his life in this world will keep it for eternal life. If any one serves me, he must follow me; and where I am there shall my servant be also; if anyone serves me, the Father will honor him. (12:25–26, RSV)

Discipleship in John's Gospel is not simply a matter of passive receptivity to God's revelation, simply a question of "seeing and believing." It demands a living out of Jesus' words and deeds: "If you remain in my word you are truly my disciples, and you shall know the truth and the truth will free you" (8:31–32). Typically, all of these themes come together explicitly in Jesus' farewell to his disciples, which is also obviously a message to the readers of the Gospel:

> This is my commandment, that you love one another as I have loved you. Greater love has no man than this, to lay down his life for his friends. You are my friends if you do what I command you. No longer do I call you servants, for the servant does not know what his master is doing; but I have called you friends, for all that I have heard from the Father I have made known to you. You did not choose me but I chose you and appointed you that you should go and bear fruit and that your fruit should abide; so that whatever you ask the Father in my name, he may give it to you. This I command you, to love one another. (15:12–17, RSV)

Despite the many differences between the Fourth Gospel and the Synoptics—differences that are real and that resist harmonization—and despite the distinctive shaping of the image of Jesus as the revealer of God in the world, we find in this narrative recognizably the same Jesus we have encountered throughout the New Testament. In his ministry, he demonstrates a pattern of obedience to God his Father that is spelled out by self-giving to others: he pours out the Spirit by himself experiencing thirst. And he calls his followers to an imitation of that same pattern.

CHAPTER 12

The Continuing Mystery

Christian spirituality is not a matter of cultivating a certain part of ourselves that we call "spirit," or of achieving a state of psychic serenity untouched by the confusion and suffering inflicted by those "others" who surround us in the world. It is instead a matter of engaging with our freedom that which is very much "other" to us: God's Holy Spirit. It therefore also entails encountering—or better, being encountered by—the one who has become "life-giving Spirit": our Lord Jesus Christ. Christian spirituality is gospel-centered, meaning that it is defined by the good news from God concerning what God has accomplished in Jesus and consists in a process of learning Jesus in a manner that transforms our lives according to the pattern of his own.

The argument of this book has been that this process of learning is necessarily both *continuous* and *complex*, because it requires not answering questions about a dead person in the past but relating to the mystery of a living person in the present.

The process of learning Jesus is *continuous* because Jesus, as a living person, continues to act and speak in the world through the Holy Spirit and through a variety of embodiments. (See chapters 1–3.) Having a living faith means responding at every moment to the living God: thus the process of learning Jesus involves coming to know him in the present as well as learning about him in the past.

If faith were merely learning about Jesus as a dead person in the past, there could at some point be an end to it. But since faith is a response to the living Lord who presses upon us at every moment, there is no time at which we can quit without betraying the entire process in which we have been engaged.

The process of learning Jesus is also *complex*. Earlier I suggested that philosophical traditions in the West have tended to favor simplicity and univocal presentation. In other words, truth is connected to unity, opinion to multiplicity. This perspective affects the learning of Jesus in two important ways: by suppressing the complexity of the process of learning itself and by suppressing the complexity of the images of Jesus. This dual tendency distorts the truth of personal and intersubjective learning, which is always multiple and complex.

The desire to find, declare, and propagate a simple and univocal Jesus who "matches" an individual believer (or some group of believers) perfectly—and without remainder—is in this instance idolatrous, since it exchanges the difficult and challenging truth for a counterfeit version that is more comfortable. But by "truth" I do not mean some other single image of Jesus that is better than those being proposed. I mean instead the truth of the *process* of personal and intersubjective learning. In the case of Jesus, such learning is complex because it involves both textual and nontextual sources, and because each of these sources, in turn, involves a variety of elements.

We saw in the first part of this book how each person's learning of Jesus takes place within a communal context that itself has many dimensions. The church as the body of the risen Christ articulates its identity through the canon of Scripture, the rule of faith, and its teaching authority; thus learning Jesus within the church means learning him within the framework called "tradition." Tradition also includes, however, the multiple embodiments of the risen Lord through which Jesus continues to call, confront, and challenge a church that otherwise might be content to rest within the security of its received self-definition.

In the practice of worship, in the lives of the saints, and in the reception of strangers, Jesus continues to encounter and challenge the church in powerful and sometimes provocative ways. The community context for learning Jesus not only serves a stabilizing function by compensating for the excesses of private or idiosyncratic learning through dialogue and discernment within the assembly of believers; it also serves a generative function: the Holy Spirit is at work in the lives of all so that the learning of Jesus within the church is both interactive and intersubjective.

Nothing could be more obvious than that such a process of learning involves a considerable amount of ambiguity. No small part of the suffering that is intrinsic to discipleship is the stress and tension attendant upon a constant need to grow into a larger awareness without being certain of either the precedents or the consequences of such growth. Ambiguity is not the same as formlessness or arbitrariness, however. Ambiguity is the element of tentativeness, of risk, of gamble, in committing to a path of understanding and action that is definite but also open-ended. If the church is committed to learning Jesus as a living person, then it is also committed to ambiguity as an inevitable—and positive!—dimension of its existence. The effort to close this conversation is, in effect, a sin against the Holy Spirit.

In the second portion of this book, we have found an equally complex situation in the compositions of the New Testament, which present a diversity of images of Jesus. We are not surprised, for we know that the New Testament was composed out of a process of learning Jesus at least as complex as that we experience in the contemporary church, and that its writings are best appreciated as witnesses and interpretations of the same mystery with which the contemporary church finds itself involved: the mystery of God's transformative work through the crucified and raised Messiah, Jesus. The compositions of the New Testament were written by participants in the same mystery who were distinguished by their historical and social circumstances. The respective situations and perspectives therefore help shape the witness and interpretation of Jesus found in each New Testament document. To commit ourselves to learning Jesus within the context of the tradition of the church, therefore, is to resist the temptation to select only one set of compositions as authoritative, or one image of

Jesus as exclusively authentic and normative, as well as the temptation to seek a "historical Jesus" standing apart from the witness and interpretation of these compositions of faith.

The diversity of images of Jesus in the New Testament is indeed dazzling. What multiple associations are generated by each of the separate titles given to Jesus in these writings: teacher, Messiah, king, prophet, priest, Lord, Son of man, Son of God, first-born of the dead, amen, Savior, redeemer, servant, Righteous One, Son of David, Word, overseer, judge, advocate, witness, friend. And how much more complex those associations become when put into a variety of combinations by each composition. There are also the many metaphors and metonymies applied to Jesus— lamb, shepherd, door, vine, light, bread, water, blood, temple, spirit, anchor, stone, builder—which are also combined in intricate ways. It is impossible to select one of these titles or metaphors as more central than the others. They are all put in play by the compositions themselves for our learning of Jesus. None of them captures all of Jesus; none is without some truth concerning Jesus. We are incredibly enriched precisely by their abundance and diversity, and we would be impoverished by the loss of any of them.

We have seen as well that the image of Jesus is affected by the purpose and genre of each composition: in the epistolary literature of the New Testament (including Revelation), it is the living presence of Jesus as Lord that is most explicit, with attention to his human ministry left largely implicit; in the Gospels, Jesus' human ministry is obviously the explicit focus, with the perspectives and concerns of the postresurrection church largely implicit. Yet each of the Gospel narratives shapes its image differently: Mark's emphasis on Jesus as the suffering Son of man is not the same as Matthew's emphasis on Jesus as teacher of the church or Luke's emphasis on Jesus as the prophet like Moses or John's emphasis on Jesus as the revealer of the Father.

This diversity of witness and interpretation is real. There truly is a "different" Jesus in each of the New Testament writings. The Jesus of Paul and the Jesus of Revelation have distinct characteristics, the Jesus of Hebrews looks different from the Jesus of James. Mark and John do not witness to Jesus identically; the interpretations of Jesus in Matthew and John are not the same. Attempts to deny or suppress this rich diversity for the sake of a simple or univocal understanding of Jesus require that violence be done to the very compositions that bear witness to him and interpret him.

At the same time, our survey of these writings has brought to light an equally remarkable and unmistakable convergence on certain aspects of Jesus' identity—not always, of course, in the same fashion or in the same proportion. Nowhere in the New Testament writings, for example, is Jesus simply a figure of the past who is remembered because of the things he said and did. Jesus is everywhere a figure whose past words and deeds are remembered because and in light of his present and continuing power. The present power of Jesus as risen Lord, moreover, anticipates his future role as triumphant judge of the living and the dead. In one way or another, the New Testament writings witness to Jesus as sharing in the life and power of God.

Given such a strong sense of Jesus as Lord, the attention paid to Jesus' humanity in the New Testament is the more impressive. We find it not only in the narratives about his past but equally in letters emphasizing his present divine power. In none of these writings is Jesus' humanity either subsumed by a process of divinization or forgotten. In all of them, his humanity stands as the measure of Christian life and identity. His words are commandments that the church not only preserves but seeks to obey. His acts anticipate and express the power that the church recognizes as still active in the community of faith. Above all, however, it is the *character* of the human person Jesus that remains normative for believers. It is not the incidentals of his unique historical existence—his Jewishness, maleness, and habits of speech—that are transferable to others, but the pattern of his life, the way in which he disposed of his freedom: this "mind of Christ" is replicable in the freedom of other humans through the power of the Holy Spirit.

It is on this point, in fact, that we find the most consistent testimony in the writings of the New Testament—namely, that there is a necessary congruence between the character of Jesus' human life and the character of Christian discipleship.

Nowhere in the New Testament is there an image of the human Jesus that is compatible with attitudes of hubris, hedonism, envy, arrogance, acquisitiveness, self-aggrandizement, hostility, or violence. Jesus is everywhere associated with faithful obedience toward God and meek, compassionate, self-emptying service toward other people.

Jesus' character reveals him to be someone who hopes in the power of God rather than in human manipulation, who faithfully obeys God rather than his own project, and who loves with a self-giving of time and energy and presence to the needs of others in preference to his own.

That is why the cross of Jesus stands as the central symbol for his entire life: his death was in faithful obedience to God even when he wanted to live; his death was an act of love to overcome alienation between humans; his death was the ultimate expression of hope in a God who can call into being that which does not exist and can therefore give life to the dead.

Similarly, we find nowhere in the New Testament an understanding of Christian discipleship compatible with a life devoted to one's own success, pleasure, comfort, freedom from suffering, or power at the expense of others. Everywhere we find the qualities that are found in Jesus advanced as essential to the following of Jesus: the same faith, the same love, the same hope. The basic pattern of faithful obedience to God and loving service to others is the image of Christ that the Spirit replicates in the freedom of those who belong to Christ.

Although I have suggested that an openness to learning Jesus in all of life's complex situations means that the church is committed to ambiguity as a basic dimension of its existence, there is no ambiguity to be found in this basic pattern. It is the pattern enacted in baptism and the eucharist. It is the pattern expressed by the creed. It is the pattern recognized in the lives of the saints. The imitation of Christ in his life of service and suffering—not as an act of masochism for the sake of suppressing one's own life but as an act of love for the enhancement of others' life—is not an optional version of Christian identity. It is the very *essence* of Christian identity. It is the pattern by which every other claim about the spiritual life must be measured if it is to be considered Christian. It is what is learned from Jesus. It is what learning Jesus means.

Learning by Living

In an earlier chapter I cautioned readers not to confuse my analysis of the Gospels with the sort of reading demanded by the process of learning Jesus. Likewise, reading a book about spirituality is not the same as engaging the Holy Spirit of God with one's own freedom. The same elements involved in all intersubjective learning are required for learning Jesus.

This is not a matter of having casual opinions about who Jesus might have been. It is not a matter of reaching scientifically verifiable conclusions about who Jesus must have been. It is rather a matter of learning a living person, and through that process being transformed in one's own identity.

The claim to be learning Jesus is superficial if not grounded in specific practices that embody such learning. The pattern of faithful obedience and loving service is not something to be memorized as though it were a mental image. Rather, it is a pattern that must be spelled out in the practices of living faith within a community. The pattern by which we were imprinted by baptism—the pattern of a dying and rising Lord Jesus—is etched ever more deeply in us when at the Lord's Supper we share the body of the Lord given for us and the blood of the Lord poured out for us. It is impressed on us also by those saints with whom we live and who have nourished us in the faith by their lives of obedience and selfless love. It is reinforced for us as well by reading and meditating together in Scripture that talks of Jesus' own self-disposition in faith and love.

We need also, however, to translate this pattern into consistent habits of behavior that express the mind of Christ. We shall not be able to learn Jesus in the sick and imprisoned unless we visit those who are sick and imprisoned. We shall not find Jesus in the hungry and thirsty unless we go to those who are hungry with food and those who are thirsty with drink. We shall not meet Jesus in the stranger unless we provide the stranger with hospitality.

And we shall not have the strength or purity of heart to engage the world in this fashion if we do not in the name of Jesus spend time in silent prayer and meditation on the mysteries of his life and death and resurrection. We shall not have the courage to open our hearts and homes unless we practice the sharing of our possessions in a disciplined and discerning fashion. We shall not be able to distinguish between Jesus and the fantasies of our own ideal self-image unless we purify our hearts and clarify our perception through the practice of fasting.

All these disciplines that school us in suffering shape in us a character that is prepared for the real risks taken by faith's freedom when in the name of Jesus it engages the larger world. While the pattern of faith and love is clear, how we should live out that pattern in specific circumstances rarely is. What does it mean to live in obedient faith in this social context, within this political system, under this economic regime, faced with these distortions of human value? What does it mean to act in loving fashion when faced with structures and systems and persons who are defined by idolatry's denial of God? For that matter, what does it mean to be faithful and loving in one's own small round of daily life? It is in this process of discernment that we need all the images of Jesus that the New Testament can provide, and as many examples as it can give us of how the pattern of the Messiah can be enacted in diverse situations.

This is why we pay attention to the saints. It is from the way in which the identity of Jesus finds new and distinctive expression in their individual lives that we gain insight into how we might also translate the mind of Christ into lives that are fully engaged with the specific circumstances in which God has placed us and where the call of God comes to us.

And this is why, finally, we pray that God might shape us into saints, so that we might become living texts speaking Jesus in the world—saints from whom others also might learn Jesus.

Index